D1250603

WITHDRAWN

EUROCOMMUNISM:
a new kind of communism?

EUROCOMMUNISM:
a new kind of communism?

ANNIE KRIEGEL

Translated from the french by
PETER S. STERN

HOOVER INSTITUTION PRESS

Stanford University   Stanford, California

This book, authored by Annie Kriegel, was originally published in France under the title *Un autre communisme?* by Librairie Hachette. © Librairie Hachette 1977. It is here translated and printed by arrangement.

Hoover Institution Publication 194

© 1978 by the Board of Trustees of the
   Leland Stanford Junior University
All rights reserved
International Standard Book Number: 0−8179−6941−1
Library of Congress Catalog Card Number: 77−92081
Printed in the United States of America

To Emmanuel

Contents

Preface

I wrote most of this book between February 15 and April 15, 1977. The French edition was completed on June 1. A small number of additions or minor corrections were made in July for the American version. In the following months, however, at least three events took place that, in my opinion, have decisively clarified the phenomenon of Eurocommunism and now permit us to decide between the different hypotheses formulated here. The first event was the Soviet reaction to the book *Eurocomunismo y estado* [Eurocommunism and the State], by Santiago Carrillo, secretary-general of the Spanish Communist party. The second was the breakup in France of the Union of the Left. And the third was the celebration in Moscow of the sixtieth anniversary of the October Revolution.

Explaining the unpardonable treatment he received in Moscow, Carrillo pointed out that "Berlinguer did not just write a book on the state and Eurocommunism." Carrillo, in fact, had been forbidden to speak; Berlinguer not only had the opportunity to take the floor in public but also had a private meeting with Brezhnev.

Carrillo's reasoning is accurate. When the June 23, 1977, issue of the Soviet weekly *Novoie Vremia* (New Times) carried a violent criticism of the book, which had just been published in Spanish, some people wrongfully interpreted this attack as the pretext for a larger-scale attack on all the Eurocommunist parties. Consequently, many were astonished that Berlinguer and Marchais did not appear troubled and did not provide more than limited support for their Iberian colleague.

It was certainly plausible to imagine that the Soviets had chosen Carrillo as the sacrificial victim, rather than Berlinguer or Marchais, or all three at the same time, by making a traditional tactical calculation based on the relative strengths of the three. Instead of making a frontal attack against all possible manifestations of Eurocommunism—which would have had the unhappy effect of showing that Eurocommunism existed and would therefore contribute to bringing about its existence—it may have been expedient to take on one wing of the army that had strayed from the main force and gone out in the open on its own.

The Italian Communist party was more or less protected by its territorial contiguity with Tito's Yugoslavia, an inevitable future hot spot. The Italian party, moreover, holds too many positions of power in what remains of the Italian state to be treated as one of those inconsequential Communist parties that are not in power and show little likelihood of gaining power in the foreseeable future. As for the French Communist party, the major strategic divergence that it has undertaken in the past two years vis-à-vis the Soviet Communist party—wanting no longer to be the most determined opposition party in Gaullist-Giscardian France, but rather to be the leading force in a political alternative—was at the time much too pronounced and concrete to be camouflaged under ideology. To attack the Spanish Communist party, in contrast, would not be of great consequence; and this is all the more true because the Spanish party has just been weakened by severe reverses in the first legislative elections, receiving less than 10 percent of the votes. The Spanish Communist party remains quite fragile and marginal, especially compared with its neighbor, the Portuguese Communist party, whose orthodoxy is provocative, fierce, and vigorous.

While plausible, however, this explanation is inexact, as a careful reading of the *Novoie Vremia* article made clear. Santiago Carrillo had become the lone target because, unlike Enrico Berlinguer and Georges Marchais, he had raised the discussion from the acceptable level of strategic and political evaluation to the unacceptable level of doctrinal revision. He had postulated the existence of some new kind of communism. But "communism, real, scientific communism," wrote *Novoie Vremia*, "is unique." Here we find the common denominator of all orthodoxy—the untouchable nature of doctrine and, as well, the material sign of heresy—the erroneous book against the book of truth.

Is Carrillo a heretic? If we take as the criterion the general disorder that characterizes a mind that has recently broken from its established frame of reference, the answer is yes. The impression of being in an experimental laboratory, which one feels in reading Carrillo, is no doubt the same feeling one has in reading Lenin's most enigmatic work, *The State and Revolution*. Is this because both deal with the central mystery, the state, which is, to politics, the same sacred core that the one God is to all monotheistic religions? Is this because both Lenin and Carrillo provide foundations for new orthodoxies rather than respectful commentaries on sacrosanct texts?

To be sure, Carrillo is not Lenin; he is probably not at ease in a theoretical role, as his weakness of cluttering his work and his thoughts with the precious refinements of Parisian Marxism reveals. But Lenin was hardly more at ease in philosophy, and he did not let this bother him.

For nearly two years the world has puzzled over Eurocommunism: is it a flighty creature, or does it have real substance? If the latter is true, does it emerge from Carrillo's book as something identifiable—likely to be differentiated as a distinct variety of the Communist family? This does not appear to be the case—on the contrary, Carrillo reveals it all the more clearly for what it is—a *temptation*.

It is a temptation to escape from the ruins of Stalinism—from the Stalinism of the USSR (causing the thousands of retouchings applied to the triumphant image of the Soviet Union and the socialist world); from the Stalinism of Europe (causing the hundreds of revisions of Communist party histories, to correct everything that had abusively been turned into legend); and from the Stalinism engrained in the system of thought and the practices of each militant (causing a mad rush to insecurity, which carries with it the promise of truth and freedom).

All this is very worthwhile and meaningful in terms of symbolic value. But is it important? Does it matter today, or tomorrow, either here or in the Soviet Union? We must recall that *all* the Eurocommunist-labeled parties went to Moscow and rallied around Brezhnev in the first week of November 1977, thereby demonstrating their sense of belonging and fundamental loyalty. Consequently, it would not be possible to view Eurocommunism as the Western counterpart of the Chinese schism. The Chinese understood this right away and publicly stated that Eurocommunism is not an already stabilized variety of the Communist family, and that the process of differentiation represented by Eurocommunism in relation to the original Leninist model does not seem to lead to the eventual creation of either a distinct Communist variety or even of an independent regional Communist force.

If Eurocommunism has any existence at all, it is as a peripheral part of the Communist world, characterized by the fact that the Western system of ideas and values has shown itself capable of making inroads into local Communist parties, piercing the protective bulkhead, the "chalk circle" within which the Communist world has succeeded for half a century in shutting in even the Communist parties of the democratic societies. This weakening of doctrinal cohesion in the "Eurocommunist" sector of the Communist world is indeed a weakness that adds, in ideological terms, to the weaknesses that have previously been noted in the domain of economic affairs in the Socialist countries. Although this weakness is beyond dispute, it is not yet a mortal one, especially since it offers something tangible in exchange: the parties that have been "Eurocommunized" have been driven to bring themselves up to date by the pressures of their environment, to modernize their programs, and to become more capable, in turn, of influencing their environment.

Moreover, it is because Eurocommunism exists only within such narrow limits, defined by what in essence are negative terms, that Brezhnev has the luxury of ignoring it as such, taking a specific stance instead toward each party encompassed by the label. In dealing with the Italian Communist party, he is coaxing, wheedling; with the Spanish Communist party, he expresses calculated outrage. But as has always been the case in the sixty-year history of relations between Moscow and communism in Western Europe, most of the energy Brezhnev expends to impose his law is directed at the French Communist party. This does not mean that we can hold the Soviet party directly responsible for the breakup of the Union of the Left; it did nothing more than make known the view that it would not be overjoyed by the eventual formation of a Socialist-led government in Paris.

Its wishes have been granted. The collapse of any possibility in the near future of participation in the French government thrusts the French Communist party away from its national dimension and back toward its international dimension. While Romanian-style national communism is workable for a party in power, it does not provide sufficient legitimacy for a party thrust back upon itself. These developments support the notion that the French style of Eurocommunism was nothing more than the sum total of the adjustments made necessary by a strategy of victory for the Union of the Left. It has been pointed out that Georges

Marchais's speech to the last Central Committee meeting, on November 10, 1977, was one of the most polished of his career; this is because it was also one of the most conventional speeches he has delivered, by which I mean, in conformity with the most deep-rooted image that the Communist party has of itself.

November 12, 1977   Annie Kriegel

Introduction: Change

There is something both thrilling and trying about watching the birth pangs of a new type of politics. Such an event is indeed rare, because the political domain, more than other arenas, seems destined for a limited number of types. In a vigorous and thriving democracy each year sees the emergence and evanescence of new political groups, movements, and parties. Whether they endure or vanish, they are not—or, in most cases, were not—anything more than the products of an already established and recognized type of politics.

When the French Socialist party began its rebuilding task in 1969, it was merely fulfilling its destiny to occupy the political space that belonged to it as a matter of right. France's history, cultural tradition, social and economic structures, and political scene fully warranted a renascent Socialist party. It was but an accident, and a repairable one, that France had lost its Socialist party. Although there was no surety from the start that the rebuilding operation would succeed, and although it was necessary to see what the bearing, substance, and dimensions of this new offshoot of the Socialist family would be, the basic ingredients of the new movement were definable from the outset. It was even clear in advance that the new party could only be a left-Socialist party.

The formation of a Catholic party—the MRP—after the Liberation was another story, one that appeared to refute the long-held opinion that French political culture would not allow religious affiliation to serve as the overt basis for a political venture. But the illusion, nevertheless, was brief: The MRP did not survive the Fourth Republic. This came as no surprise, since the MRP was nothing more than the French version of the Christian Democratic parties that flourished in the large neighboring countries. It could not acclimatize itself in France.

Eurocommunism, by contrast, is a completely different phenomenon. At issue is whether an established and fully developed party with well-defined characteristics will be able to dismantle itself, right down to the essential core that has enabled it to survive for so long, and then rebuild itself out of a new concept of politics around a new essential core.

This fascinating development had hardly begun before it was the subject of a wave of speculation and commentary. Analyses were often hasty and inconsistent, as illustrated by the following commentary, chosen at random from a deluge of nonsense:

> As for Eurocommunism, for a long time there have been Western Communist parties that conducted independent policies. The Spanish party is the best example. Thus defined, Eurocommunism has always existed. But it has developed a great deal in the past few years for a number of reasons: new generations have come of age in Western Communist parties; it is perceived that "socialism" in Eastern Europe has been a relative failure; and there is a desire to share governmental power, which has led the Western parties to accept, more or less, the ground rules of the Western systems. A tactical change? Perhaps. But there's no backing off now (Jacques Huntzinger, *Le Monde*, February 20, 1977).

Not one of these categorical statements holds up. "For a long time" the Western Communist parties have "conducted independent policies"? Since when? Which parties? What policies? Can we really use the Spanish Communist party [SCP] as "the best example"? Perhaps we could, but only if the Spanish party had been involved in politics as briefly as Jacques Huntzinger has been. Have Western Communist parties really accepted "the ground rules of the Western systems"? That is the crux of the whole problem, and François Mitterrand would certainly breathe a lot easier if he could share this lighthearted evaluation.

Even the more seasoned observers hesitate. Some developments delight them, while others displease them. Generally they remain skeptical. Experienced observers vacillate between the poles of optimism and dismay as they consider Eurocommunism's chances of developing and as they speculate on its degree of maturation and its real objectives.

Take Milovan Djilas, for example. This former close friend of Marshal Tito and the theoretician of the "New Class" stated during an interview for West German television on March 2, 1977, that Eurocommunism was "the most significant European event since the Cold War." Moreover,

Djilas considered the emergence an accomplished fact: "The situation created by Eurocommunism cannot be undone."

On the very next day, however, Michel Roccard, one of the leaders of the French Socialist party, announced on France-Inter radio that "Eurocommunism doesn't mean anything, and if it has any meaning at all, it is of limited significance. It means only that for many Communist parties, especially the three major ones in Western Europe, ties with Moscow are no longer ties of discipline and obedience. These ties are now simply those of an old friendship."

Two days later, *Le Monde* (March 5) offered an evasive and predictably middle-of-the-road evaluation: "The Madrid meeting of Berlinguer, Carrillo, and Marchais has sanctioned Eurocommunism—not as a doctrine or an organizational principle—but as a state of mind." But what does a "state of mind" amount to? That's not saying much at all!

How should we proceed if we want to reach a judgment that is something more than a subjective impression? What indicators should we use to find the site and measure the extent of the break with the old politics? What criteria should we choose to size up what has been taken from the old politics, borrowed, and outwardly changed, or rethought from the ground up? How shall we measure the capacity of these retooled elements to mesh with a new type of politics? How compatible are the old and the new elements, and how coherent is their product? And, since everything points to the conclusion that the process is as yet unfinished, what factors would forward or hinder its chances to reach maturity, and how long might that take?

It is all the more urgent to devise a method of analysis, for *change* is always on the horizon of the Communist world. Change, of course, affects all human activity in every period of history, but the Communist world—more than any other—favors change over continuity, if for no other reason than its relative youth. As a philosophy of history, Marxism is a philosophy of change based upon conflict. Its ultimate objective, and central purpose, the revolution, is a radical procedure for breaking with the old in order to overcome it, not just to establish a regime of justice but to set in place a "new society," a "new man."

For their part, those who study communism want to return this strange, foreign, troubling, and exotic phenomenon to a more familiar setting. We never hear them shout "There's a change" when a Communist party in the process of contraction withdraws into itself and goes into exile within its own national political system. On the other hand, when a Communist party "leaves its ghetto" in better times and deals with the everyday world, the specialists immediately claim that it is no longer the same—it is no longer itself. Similarly, people are flabbergasted whenever a Communist acts like a normal person, as if being Communist somehow prevents him from sharing ordinary human attributes.

So we have to make clear what we are talking about when we discuss change in a Communist party (singular) or the development of Eurocommunism as the expression of change on the part of several Western European Communist parties. Where, between the inevitable phenomenon of aging and the radical—but improbable—metamorphosis does the change we are talking about take place? In the continuum of change from perception of the potentiality to the subsequent attainment of full actualization, where does the Eurocommunist phenomenon fit? In which of the three categories of change discussed below is it most at home?

Is it the kind of change that every being encounters, springing forth from exploring the boundaries of its own being, from the discovery of previously unknown possibilities within its genetic potential, from the determination with which it plans to bring in the new as efficiently as possible, within the limits of its logic and history? This is the kind of change that Georges Marchais had in mind when he repeated so frequently and with so much conviction, "We will change to better ourselves." This is the kind of change that by definition is within the boundaries of one's own being and remains compatible with its continuity.

Or is it rather the kind of change that takes place during the continuous adaptation by any being to an ever-changing environment? Here again there is nothing surprising, for this kind of change is the very condition of remaining vital or is, at least, the indicator of one's ability to find in one's own environment the nourishment that fends off apathy and allows one to continue to act and react.

Finally, is it the kind of change that produces a complete break, not merely a partial tear or snag? Is it the kind of change that signifies repudiation of what one has been, that means one is regretful and has suffered from what one has been or done and now wants to be and do something else, to repair the damage of the past? This kind of change implies stepping entirely out of one's self. We must avoid extremes of fantasy in this analysis, for the cultural order is as exempt from total metamorphosis as is the biological order. It would be unreasonable to expect that a Leninist endeavor could be entirely "de-Leninized," purged of itself, and emptied of everything that might stem from the old way. Such an analysis would be a fruitless exercise in polemics; here, we can only be concerned with measuring the degree to which the initial genetic code has been dismantled.

By taking this approach, we can avoid two methodological traps. The first trap is to waste too much time on the "sincerity" of the men and parties that carry the Eurocommunist label. As in any human endeavor, there is deception involved here—and self-deception. But as in any human endeavor, not everything is under the control of will power. It is significant to note that the French, Italian, and Spanish leaders sincerely *desire* to change. But into what are they *capable* of changing? At what price? And what risks are they willing to run?

We can also avoid the second trap, which is to attempt an *instrumental* analysis of the *sense* of Eurocommunism: In whose interest is it? Does it serve American imperialism, European capitalism, German Social-Democrats, reformers, revisionists, or authentic revolutionaries who may have found the secret of a promising detour leading up the path to power? Could Eurocommunism be a plot—a maneuver of the international bourgeoisie to create divisions in the international Communist movement? That is what Herbert Mies, the chairman of the [West] German Communist party, thinks. There is nothing that would automatically rule out such an analysis or the arguments in its favor. It will be necessary eventually to understand Eurocommunism as a reality for which all forces must establish policies—the socialist world, China, the European governments, the American administration, Soviet dissidents, and, of course, the French and Italian voters.

Right now the most urgent task is to conduct an inquiry that questions neither the sense nor the use of Eurocommunism but that aims instead at its very being: Does Eurocommunism exist? If so, what is it?

There remains a final question, the most difficult one. There will be change, of course, but when, and at what pace?

About ten years ago, in writing of the French Communist party [FCP] during the aftermath of the Red Army's invasion of Czechoslovakia, I concluded:

> It's not "we" who ask "you" to be Communists no longer; it's you who
> ask it of yourselves. Will the French Communist Party remain true to

itself, condemning itself to become a dead star, since the warmth of the hearth that was the Soviet Revolution can no longer give it life? Will the party break the chains that tie it to its nature, disgorge the stopped-up pipes of its memory, and seize the reins that bind it to the realities of the last part of the twentieth century? This is the way the world Communist movement and the French left can get back on the track and rediscover their mutual attraction, which has been lost for some time. In spite of the circumspect style and wily prudence of Waldeck-Rochet's initiative, and in spite of the predictable detours, delays, and backsliding, this is what the position taken by the French Politburo in response to the invasion of Czechoslovakia by the Red Army seems to mean. But things have to move quickly; it's not enough for Communism to change—it has to change *in time*.

On an August day twenty-nine years after the August day on which the German-Soviet pact was made public, one kind of Communism has reached its end. Now a new chapter is beginning. What will be carried over from the old one, and what will simply fade away? This book may be helpful if it can shed some light on where the nodal points are; if it can make a contribution from the outside to the birth of something that responds to the needs of a party that no longer shows scorn for socialism, freedom, and modernity. [*Les Communistes français*, Paris: Editions du Seuil, 1968, p. 256]

That was fairly well perceived, but, of course, that was ten years ago. Who in our own time has ever held that things move quickly?

1

Three Definitions

The word "Eurocommunism" is of recent vintage. Vadim Zagladin, the assistant secretary of the foreign policy section of the Central Committee of the Soviet Communist party, suspects Zbigniew Brzezinski, President Carter's National Security Affairs adviser, of being its inventor. Others point to Arrigo Levi, the editor in chief of *La Stampa* [Turin], as the creator of the expression in a *Newsweek* article, but it is probably Frane Barbieri, a Yugoslav journalist, who coined it. Newsmen seem to have launched the expression during the winter of 1975–76. It was then taken up by some Western Communist leaders, but always enclosed in quotation marks. Jean Terfve, the vice-chairman of the Belgian Communist party, used it this way in an editorial in *Le Soir* [Brussels] on January 6, 1976. Enrico Berlinguer was the first to use the word in a Communist meeting—at the European conference in Berlin in June 1976. An entire year went by before the French Communist party used the word except indirectly—by citing an article title from a non-Communist paper, as Francette Lazard did in *L'Humanité* on November 18, 1976, or in answering a direct question in a press conference, as Georges Marchais did on several occasions. It was on February 13, 1977, that Marchais indicated his approval when he stated: "We didn't invent the word, but it doesn't bother me in the least." The Soviet Communist party and the parties in the people's democracies, by contrast, have never accepted the expression.

What does this new expression mean? First, of course, it refers to a geographical area, grouping together the Communist parties of Europe and conferring on them unique characteristics. But as a geographical demarcation, its frontiers for the moment are unclear and subject to relocation. Eurocommunism is not strictly a European entity, because the Communist party of Australia has become associated with it (although we should recall that Moscow has long ago withdrawn its recognition of the Australian party). Moreover, the Japanese Communist party is even more readily identified with the term, as shown by Georges Marchais's conspicuous trip to Tokyo, taken just after he had defined his new line at the Twenty-second Congress of the FCP in February 1976. Eurocommunism is not a pan-European fact, either, since it concerns only Western Europe. In Eastern Europe, even the Romanian and Yugoslav parties, which are the standard bearers of autonomy vis-à-vis Moscow, have not accepted the new designation. Furthermore, the expression does not even take in all of Western Europe. Many of the parties there openly object to it—in Portugal, Luxemburg, West Germany, Denmark, Austria, Greece, Cyprus, and Finland. Others stay on the sidelines, refusing any designation other than that of their national territory: Iceland's Communist party is an example. The Communist party of Great Britain maintains that it has been "Eurocommunist" for twenty-five years, citing its significantly titled program from 1954, *The British Path toward Socialism,* which called for taking power within the limits of the constitution and without having recourse to civil war. At the time, however, observers paid much more attention to the fact that *Pravda* printed the entire document. Then we come to the paradoxical Communist party of the Netherlands. Known as the black sheep of the European Communist family, it has abruptly fallen into line. After having followed an independent path since 1941, it sent an official delegation to Moscow in April 1977—for the first time in fourteen years.

While it should also note that the small Irish and Belgian Communist parties view the Eurocommunist idea with favor, our survey of European communism finds that the term really concerns only three parties—those of Spain, France, and Italy. Therefore Eurocommunism appears to be the offshoot of the Mediterranean type of socialism that took shape momentarily during the life of that other supranational family, the Socialist International. The Latin background, the predominance of the Counter-Reformation type of Catholicism, the experience of the Enlightenment, a delayed industrialization process, a weak propensity for political and social democracy, the fascist experience, the centralization of the nation-state under challenge from virulent or chronic regionalism, and an old and authentic native and libertarian working-class movement—these characteristics of the three countries give them a sense of common destiny and show how real the distinction is between northern and southern Europe.

But the word Eurocommunism, beyond its geocultural meaning, is intended to convey something theoretical, ideological, and political. What? We're confronted with three possible approaches.

First approach: Eurocommunism might be a new variety of communism. The political system founded by the Russian Bolsheviks—Leninism, to use the official term—has produced a number of distinctive varieties—Stalinism, Trotskyism, Maoism, Titoism, Castroism—whose originality is measured by comparing them to the standard, the first Leninist model, which is, of course, the Soviet model. Using this approach Eurocommunism would be one more of these varieties. Its first characteristic would be that it has regional scope, in contrast with the other varieties, whose names betray their single-country scope, be it a large country (China) or a small one (Cuba). Its second characteristic would be that it represents the solution to a major preoccupation—reconciling socialism with freedom. Georges Marchais used a felicitious phrase to describe this: "[Eurocommunism] can be defined as the resemblance between the situations our parties are in and the resemblance between the responses each of our parties puts forth in order to achieve a socialist society and a democratic kind of socialism" (*L'Humanité*, February 14, 1977). Seen in this light, we may wonder whether Eurocommunism is really a new variety, since it was largely inspired by the "communism with a human face" of the "Prague Spring."

Second approach: Rather than being a new variety of the Communist family, Eurocommunism might be only a revolutionary strategy for the conquest of power on the regional level. This definition is not without ambiguity. On one hand, a regional strategy could be a simple strategy of sectors whose relative autonomy is based on the technical necessity of adapting to the peculiarities of the region in question within the worldwide strategy, which remains essential and dominant. On the other hand, a regional strategy could also develop an autonomous and independent logic of its own, one that would no longer have to fit within a larger strategy that controls it. By appearing to be an informal grouping up to now, either, at a minimum, as a regional grouping within the worldwide Communist movement that "tries to deal with problems common to its members," or, at a maximum, as a regional replacement for a worldwide Communist movement in state of collapse, Eurocommunism could be trying to modify the traditional level of revolutionary initiative, which for sixty years has been like a ladder with only two rungs—the world level and the national level. Such an interpretation, if true, would tend to confirm the general tendency in our time toward a decline of worldwide systems and of the nation-states to the profit of less institutionalized *regional* systems at the supranational and infranational levels.

Third approach: Eurocommunism might be neither a fully developed variety of the Communist family nor a regional strategy. Instead, it could aim in a more limited manner at being only an inclination—or, better yet, a temptation—shared by some Communist parties. It could principally represent a negative attempt of the parties to establish some distance between themselves and the Soviet component of communism. But it could also be a positive endeavor to find, after so many debates on Asian Marxism, after so many experiences with proletarian revolution in exotic peasant societies, what could be the originality of Leninist revolutions in Western Europe: that of being revolutions in industrial societies that have sociologically definable working classes. In brief, Eurocommunism could be the Communist effort to participate in the overall European struggle to find reality and identity. This would be proof that revolutionary politics, in which Europe has been the leader for over two centuries, still have vitality.

2

Whose Fault Is It?

Before examining the implications of these three possible approaches to Eurocommunism, let us review briefly the factors that may have contributed to the emergence of this phenomenon.

We must certainly not ignore the pressures exerted both now and in the past against world communism, pressures that strive to weaken it or break it up, by various elements of the political systems, economic development, and culture of the societies and states of Western Europe. As William E. Griffith has pointed out, the long period of global stabilization, peace, and prosperity enjoyed by Western Europe since 1945— which culminated during the 1960s in détente between East and West— has had the same effect on communism as the long period of peace after the Franco-Prussian War had on the German Social-Democratic party.

The establishment of the European Economic Community, which has been partly successful, has also brought pressure on the unity and homogeneity of the pan-European Communist movement, to which the parties involved in Eurocommunism belong. The EEC, in effect, has created a new type of solidarity that has driven a wedge between its member states and the countries of Eastern Europe, which were provoked into forming a similar grouping.

Finally, since 1974, according to most observers, the economic crisis and its social and moral corollaries, rather than détente, has been the stimulus of the Eurocommunist response. Berlinguer summed it up at the Madrid conference by saying, "Western Europe runs the risk of entering a decadent phase that could drag it into a kind of modern barbarism."

It might well be that in recent times the defense mechanisms embodied in the basic principles of Communist parties for warding off the danger of corruption by the environment have been overwhelmed or surprised. We might be witnessing the reversal of the current, a reversal that up to now has been characteristic only of social democracy: Now it is no longer socialism that penetrates the country; it is the country that penetrates socialism. This was Jaurès's formula to identify precisely the kind of phenomenon for which Rosa Luxemburg, before the First World War, coined the term *opportunism*.

But it is still necessary to explain this weakening of the guard protecting the unchanging Communist core, the guard that held at a distance and, when necessary, threw outside the "chalk circle" any unhealthy secretions from the social tissue in which it was lodged, that filtered everything coming from this tissue in order to keep only what was assimilable and compatible, whatever would allow it to be even better adapted, ready for new growth. Why, after sixty years, has this mechanism broken down and reversed itself?

To understand this we must focus on what it is that causes change inside the Communist movement and in its most important institutions. The year 1956, marked by the Twentieth Congress of the Soviet Communist Party, when Khrushchev burned his bridges by giving the famous "Secret Report" speech, brought to a sudden close the thirty-year period during which the Soviet model, after enclosing itself in the Stalinist version, had become the nearly exclusive bearer of the Leninist label. We can well understand Khrushchev's strategy: He wanted to win the loyalty of the party cadres by announcing, in this wild but entirely believable speech, an end to the Stalinist arbitrariness of which they were at that time the beneficiaries but could eventually become the victims. However, the enormous distance between the objective of this strategy— the appropriation of power—and its endless repercussions reveals, in my opinion, that the tyrant's successor had much more in mind than simply a rational strategy. Perhaps there was something in the soul of this crafty but down-to-earth peasant that brought about a rebellion of the truth, an irresistible temptation to wash away sin and shame.

In any case, the period since 1956, though marked by occasional remissions, has been rich in forward bounds and rapid progress. The immediate and nearly unanimous condemnation in August 1968 of the Soviet military intervention in Czechoslovakia by the Western European Communist parties is a good example. The uninterrupted crisis of Leninism has had effects in the socialist states that have also reached the parties of Western Europe. From Togliatti through Longo to Berlinguer in Italy, from Thorez through Waldeck-Rochet to Marchais in France, the effects of the crisis are easy to see. Since the Eighth Congress of the Italian Communist Party [ICP] in 1956, these effects have played a role in the shrewd and ambiguous development of an ongoing, coordinated movement in Italy. The high points of this movement have been the presentation of the polycentrism thesis in 1956, the rapprochement with Tito, the publication of the *Yalta Testament* in 1964, the condemnation of the Soviet invasion of Czechoslovakia in 1968, the systematic conquest of local government in all the major cities of Italy, including Rome, and finally the definition of the historic compromise.

Meanwhile, the French party experienced the usual stop-and-go politics, with wild takeoffs and hairpin turns. The style lacked graceful-ness, but this is perhaps due to the quantity of energy needed to push the cumbersome party apparatus out of its ponderous routine. It would be unjust not to give credit for this effort to Georges Marchais, even though it may be difficult to reconcile the heaviness and brutal manner reflected by his personality and career with his capacity to carry out a daringly mobile policy without losing track of the course he has set. We must be careful not to judge the book by its cover. Because Togliatti and a number of the Italian Communist party leaders were polished intellec-tuals who spoke with elegance and clothed their behavior in a mantle of cynicism, to make it less "heavy," there is a tendency to excuse them for a constancy to Stalinism that would not be permitted to Thorez and the French leaders, who have come from humble origins. Today the situation is the same; Berlinguer and his friends, most of whom are from good social backgrounds, benefit from a credit denied to Marchais and his colleagues, the majority of whom are still from modest families. The working-class share in the leadership of the Italian party fell from 40 percent to 6 percent between 1946 and 1975. After all, Mussolini was no Hitler, and Italian fascism did not sink to the bloody madness of nazism. It would seem reasonable to take account of this historical precedent in order not to draw conclusions about the real nature of things on the basis of traits drawn from Italian culture and manners and especially, using Franco Ferrarotti's expression, from the complex history of Marxism in Italy.

Against this background of a general crisis in Leninism, two new sets of factors have recently emerged. The first is expressed by the twofold modification in recent years of the image of the Soviet Union. Soviet society has indeed ceased to appear to be the "best society," i.e., the most just and the most content society; the Soviet state, on the other hand, now wields a fantastic amount of military power. The old dream of a world revolution to bring about a worldwide socialist government and

world peace seems now to be based upon a formidable capacity for
expansion. It is easy to identify the two principal forces responsible for
this reshaping of the Soviet image: the dissident Soviet intelligentsia,
both inside and outside the Soviet Union, whose many different persons,
values, and works are symbolized by the names Solzhenitsyn and
Sakharov; and China, whose obstinacy in treating the Soviet menace as
its top priority makes a strong impression.

The second set of factors is made up of the contrasting results drawn
from the fragmented, discontinuous, and dispersed manner in which,
from 1973 to 1977, the Soviet Union and the worldwide Communist
movement tried to exploit the general economic crisis of the capitalist
West and the American political crisis of Watergate. Following the
Leninist tradition, economic crisis and war are the two trigger situations
that can lead to the breaking of a "weak link" in the chains of capitalism
and imperialism. This working hypothesis has been verified by com-
parative analysis of revolutionary situations over the past three centuries,
although the economic situation that best promotes development of a
dangerous situation occurs when a downturn—even a minor one—
suddenly interrupts a long upward movement of the economic indicators. Moreover, the economic crisis that began at the end of 1973 held
more encouraging signs than some of the preceding crises. (The Great
Depression, as we know, was more propitious to fascist subversion than
to proletarian revolution.) This time the crisis was likely to continue
indefinitely, to the extent that it was fed by the energy crisis, for which no
end could be foreseen. Most of all, the economic crisis went hand in hand
with a yet more promising political crisis, although it was possible,
unfortunately, to foresee the end of the crisis, and the return to
normalcy in the American political system, by application of the constitutional processes and by the election of a new president. Because
Watergate was a political crisis, it was a general crisis that touched all
aspects of American life, including the operations of the Department of
Defense. In this doubly propitious situation, Vietnam and Angola served
to illustrate the decisive role played by the military powers of the socialist
states in winning over to the socialist camp new "liberated" territories. By
contrast, Chile, Portugal, and the Middle East underscored the *political*
inadequacy of the Communist *parties* involved.

To be sure, the three unfortunate experiences did not have the same
results, and their lessons have not had the same impact. Middle Eastern
affairs are too complex, and the conditions of political struggle there too
dissimilar to Western European politics, to allow the major failure of the

revolutionary effort in Lebanon in 1976 to cause sharp reactions on the part of the Italian and French Communist parties, in spite of the not inconsiderable efforts made by them in the summer of 1976 to spark mobilization of an international movement of solidarity in support of the "Islamo-progressives." The alliance of the Lebanese Left (in which the Lebanese Communist party played a leading role among the progressive forces) and the Palestine Liberation Organization, which, had it been successful, might have swung around the way the nationalist Castro had moved when he became a Marxist-Leninist and a faithful ally of the Soviet Union, was in no way comparable to the Union of the Left in France or the historic compromise in Italy.

On the other hand, the total catastrophe of the Chilean experience— total because it had a devastating conclusion and drew the Communist party of Chile down with it—seems to have led to reflections that were bitter, salutary, and productive, especially in the Italian Communist party. As for the Portuguese situation, the French Communist party, which from beginning to end had supported Cunhal's Soviet-approved strategy, was quite exercised by the semi-failure there. It was only a semi-failure because the adventure did produce some positive results: The Communist party was able to extricate itself from the affair intact, and the entire Portuguese empire in Africa fell into the drift of the socialist camp. In the European part of the affair, on the other hand, things didn't go as planned. This gave the French Communist party a lot to think about in the weeks that preceded its major shift in the fall of 1975.

In short, it is as if each party leadership group—in Spain, in Italy, and in France—had in turn encountered a moment when something began to move in its accumulated ideas and value system. Whether it was a moment of grace or one of surrender is unimportant. After this moment, the irenic vision was irreparably spoiled. For Carrillo, it was 1956 and the Twentieth Congress of the Soviet Communist Party. For the Italians, it was Chile in September 1973. For the French it was Portugal in the summer of 1975.

Why was it at these precise times—neither sooner nor later? Cunhal was in Prague in 1968, but he was not affected by what happened. Collective beings as well as individuals have their own histories, paces of life, and secrets. What happened in Prague in 1968 to make Roger Garaudy find intolerable what he had been able to tolerate at Budapest in 1956? The only thing we know for sure is how, not why, the clock strikes—decisively and without warning.

3

Reconciling Socialism with Freedom

Let us now examine each of the three possible definitions of Eurocommunism.

Has Eurocommunism already become a new variety of communism? Although it would be saying a lot to put the matter thus right now, we must be careful to avoid the other extreme of reducing Eurocommunism to a simple proreformist movement or to a restatement of the notion of a peaceful and parliamentary transition to socialism. These themes are certainly present in Eurocommunism, along with their corollaries—the multiparty system and the defense of civil and political liberties. But these are old themes that go back to the epoch of the Fronts and have nothing very striking about them. Eurocommunism has a higher and more comprehensive ambition: to make up for what appears today as the major Communist failing—the Communist movement's inability to integrate freedom into the socialist goal right from the start.

Again it is necessary to focus on what is new—and wanting freedom is not new. After all, Communists have never labeled themselves as supporters of a "Gulag for everyone." During the Popular Front, we might remember, Eugen Fried, who was the Communist International's representative to Maurice Thorez, suggested the slogan "The Popular Front for bread, peace, and *freedom*." And Thorez himself coined the well-known phrase "For a free, strong, and happy France." What is new is being told now that the classic socialist model was not necessarily concerned with freedom.

In this perspective there are at least four interlocking debates that open up in a more or less concomitant manner.

The first debate concerns the origins, nature, and effects of Stalinism, a debate that was practically forbidden, in the French Communist party, at least, for twenty years. Because of this long delay, the debate has taken on a theological rather than an academic tone, which is unfortunate, since it would have been preferable to use the scientific techniques (scrupulous establishment of facts, careful examination of trends, circumstances, and processes) proper to an academic setting.

Of the two competing interpretations in this debate, Jean Elleinstein's right-wing approach is certainly more valuable than the analysis of Louis Althusser. The suggestion, which Althusser makes, that Stalinism should be seen as an excessively "democratic" deviation from Leninism, as an "economist" carryover of social-democratic meanderings during the Second International, has a fascinating "doctrinal affectation" about it, in Jacques Julliard's words, but is, of course, absurd. This interpretation might also be out-and-out indecent. We have to wonder just what the Althusserian Diafoirus* of revolutionary pathology are talking about when they tell us solemnly about a "leftist interpretation" of Stalinism that seeks to "analyze the total function of the institutions and apparatus of the state—the entire juridicopolitical superstructure—from a class point of view," and when they then add abruptly: "The connivance between democracy and Stalinism is obvious. Democracy engenders its own violence because it perpetuates class relations all the way to socialism, and it must be remembered that capitalism has been able to develop only under democracy" (*Le Monde*, December 1976).

Nicos Poulantzas, who is more concerned about maintaining real political debate, stays clear of such gushing metaphysics, but how can he aspire to greater clarity when he begins by attributing to a disavowed Stalin what is really due to Lenin? When he writes, "The Communist party is discarding a certain concept of the state passed on essentially by Stalinism, one that considers the capitalist state as a monolithic and unbroken edifice run at will by the bourgeoisie, which can be seized by a frontal assault and can be destroyed by a dual-power type of situation" (*Le Monde*, March 1977), he is analyzing something that is not from Stalin, and, moreover, it was under Stalin that the alternative strategy of the Popular Front was conceived. This was the substitution for the frontal assault from without (Winter Palace, 1917) of the conquest of power from within through the use of governmental power that had evolved from coalition participation (Prague, 1948).

---

* Quack doctors in Molière's *Le malade imaginaire*.

Elleinstein's undertaking is less gratuitous than Althusser's. No matter what he may think of it himself, Althusser's effort is nothing more than the personal endeavor of an ordinary philosopher. Although a member of the Communist party, he is in no way associated with its leadership. Even in the area of his expertise—Marxist theory—he is not consulted. In his case, democratic centralism seems to work backward: First the leadership of the party decided that the concept of the dictatorship of the proletariat was obsolete; then Althusser challenged this interpretation. Since he is neither associated with nor consulted by the party leaders, Althusser maintains his entire freedom of thought, of action, and of expression in the same measure that the party is entirely free with regard to him. This situation of reciprocal ignorance is unexceptional: The degree of control that the Communist party exercises over its members is not uniform, and it is not above allowing those of its supporters that can bring it esteem and fame to gambol about without having to comply with established Communist practice. All this, of course, on condition that the party is not tied down by these individuals, any more than they are tied down by the party.

Elleinstein's position is quite different. He is garbed in the trappings of a traditional academic figure. But this does not mean that he is a petit-bourgeois democrat. During the 1950s he worked for the apparatus of international communism. It is, naturally, possible that his subsequent position as historian and the rules of the game he has learned to follow in the university have led him to question the adequacy of the Stalinist version of the history of the Soviet Union. It soon became apparent that his efforts could buttress the project being worked out in the closed ranks of the FCP leadership. This is not to say that Elleinstein was immediately promoted—or demoted—to the position of informal spokesman for the party. Supported and guided by a more thorough and precocious knowledge of the leadership's intentions than was normal for someone in his hierarchical position, Elleinstein had to evaluate his status like an explorer sounding out the risks and dangers of a mission. He saw that he would be cast aside if the venture proved unsuccessful; if it worked, on the other hand, he would be brought into the group effort that was already underway. So he chose to cut his risks by taking a modest position in all senses of the term: But if the "Stalinist phenomenon" was for him only a "violation" of "social-ist legality," as a historian he felt constrained to describe the concrete elements of this violation. His readers can conclude that if there was socialist legality, it did not offer much in the way of a guarantee, and it must have been chopped to bits by the ferocious treatment it received.

In any case, behind these mostly rhetorical diagnoses one can observe a much more decisive preliminary battle shaping up on the pertinence in good Marxist-Leninist theory of the truth/falsehood dichotomy.

"If we had only known," said Jean Kanapa about the Arthur London affair, "we would have screamed in protest." What absurd pathos! By trying to clear himself, as well as his party, Kanapa comes across as a very bad actor. It would be much better if he could explain how and why the relationship of the FCP to truth and falsehood has passed through three phases during the party's lifetime.

If we had only known? It is a fact that Communists in the years prior to Stalin's death in 1953, almost without exception (Aragon was one, perhaps), and at whatever level of responsibility, even in the Soviet Union, claimed that they "did not know." Alain Besançon, for instance, remarked, "I tend to think that Stalin ignored how many people were in the Gulag . . . by several million." There is the paradox of the Stalinist world: In spite of the omnipresence of the police and the system of mutual denunciation, information was atomized and compartmentalized, even for the leaders.

The ignorance of the Communists, like that of the Nazis in the same period, was not fortuitous and personal, and the plea of ignorance was no more valid for the former than it was for the latter, because this ignorance was the product of the system. People didn't know the truth—not because they refused it, not because they did not seek it out, and not because they preferred its opposite, falsehood. No, in the Stalinist system truth was considered nothing more than an element of mystification for use by the dictatorship of the bourgeoisie. According to Stalin and his followers, it was the bourgeoisie and imperialism (of the English, French, German, Japanese, American, or Zionist variety, according to the circumstances) that wanted to make people believe there was an objective reality; but this, for Stalin, was mere "objectivism." Facts themselves were insignificant. When they were promoted to having a certain meaning, then it became only a matter of interpretations, some of which served imperialism, while others served socialism.

It was a vain exercise to pretend "not to have known." How could one have known, since there was nothing to know other than the truth of the party, and since this truth, as ideological as any other party truth, taught that the accused persons in the major political trials had been obliged to admit that they were traitors, spies, Zionists, Trotskyites, or bourgeois nationalists?

Under these conditions, those who decided to "know" (for indeed, to their honor, there were some) could do so only by leaving the system or, at least, by moving to its periphery. But then the second phase began and things changed radically after 1956 and the Twentieth Congress of the Soviet Communist Party, when Khrushchev himself revealed, in an incoherent but torrential manner, what the "truth of the party" opened onto. From that date on, the leaders of the FCP (including Jean Kanapa) were obliged to "know" in the literal sense of the word, because this knowledge was put forward by their own kind, by people authorized to pass on the "truth of the party." But the French leaders chose the path that led not from rose-colored ideological truth to somber ideological truth but from ideological truth to pure and simple falsehood. That continued for nearly twenty years. Waldeck-Rochet alone, nearly ten years ago, was smitten with the desire for truth, and he sought to free himself from the obsession of falsehood. Frightened at what he found, he submerged himself in the silence of unreason.

For the French Communist party the transition from Stalin to Khrushchev was but a painful moment when everyone worked madly to delay, postpone, and escape as long as they could from the full consequences of the revelations of the Twentieth Congress. This was the object of all French initiatives in Moscow in 1956 and after. There is irrefutable evidence that the French Communist leaders chose falsehood in its banal, naked, and direct form, without ideological trappings: In short, falsehood that is the contrary of truth. They refused to do for their own past what Khrushchev had done for his. We must remember that they had their own business to keep in order; they were not just pawns. The FCP had been a section of the Communist International, and later it had been a member of Cominform. It is too often forgotten that the purge trials in the Soviet Union and in the people's democracies had their equivalent in France: The Marty-Tillon affair in 1952 was the explicit offshoot, in France, of the Slansky trial. The French trial was a mock trial in the judicial sense, of course, since the party did not have a secular arm to do the killing (directly, anyway, for André Marty died under the blows of calumny, chagrin, and shame, and of a kind of dazed senility). When was there a full rehabilitation of the condemned persons? When did the FCP recognize the ignominy of the affair?

Now we are in the third phase, which opened in the fall of 1975; the party now recognizes that truth and reality exist, and that a supposed "party truth" cannot destroy or reject them. By means of this recognition the FCP can catch up with reality and update its own history. The turnabout was so abrupt, and was taken with such gusto, that it has prompted many questions: Is this a real desire to find truth, considering that the pursuit of truth—when one is serious about it, especially after having mocked it for so long—requires careful consideration, scrupulous, methodical doubt, and patient study?

Does the brutality of the turnabout reflect internal resistance? It was apparently necessary for Georges Marchais to interrupt his winter vacation to insist that the Politburo go back on its denials of the preceding month and recognize, in a public statement issued on January 12, 1977, that Maurice Thorez, Jacques Duclos, and the French delegation at the Twentieth Congress of the Soviet Communist Party did indeed get a copy then and there of Khrushchev's "Secret Report," and that Georges Cogniot had made a "rapid, summary, and improvised" translation of it from Russian to French.

Does Marchais want to go the whole route? During a press luncheon on January 25, 1977, when he stated, "We can say with certainty today that, after the Twenty-second Congress [of the FCP], it is unthinkable that we will not respond truthfully and publicly to any question at all," a newsman asked him, "Does that apply to all topics?" and Marchais answered, "Yes, categorically yes."

Because the word is new for them, "truth" has had an extraordinary vogue among Communists. "Truth and Hope" [*Vérité espoir*] is the title given by the cells to the campaign of drawing up grievance lists. "Truth and Change" [*Vérité changement*] is the slogan chosen for a publicity campaign for *L'Humanité*.

But while the party for the moment condemns the theory of "ideological truth," and while it abandons the practice of overall lying, it still produces only partial truths intermeshed with all kinds of falsehood—by omission, by inadvertence, by ignorance, et cetera. On the very day that he made his commitment "categorically" to truth, Marchais stated almost in the same breath, and with the same tone of conviction, "I have learned from *L'Humanité* that the Paris Communists have decided to name Henri Fiszbin, who is a deputy and a member of the Central Committee, as their leader." Is this a truthful description of the manner in which decisions of this import are made by the FCP?

And, above all, are we to imagine that the aphorism that was called upon so often by the habit of imposture—"Truth is revolutionary"— might not begin to revolutionize the Communist party itself? What real meaning can we give to the party's encouragement of historians to "evaluate our past behavior" when we hear statements like this one by Marchais, at the same press luncheon: "We are unanimous in thinking that the essential part of the policies followed by our party between its creation and the Twenty-second Congress served the best interests of socialism"?

The second debate is not on freedom per se but on civil rights and liberties in a bourgeois democracy. This subject first came up in Communist policy as an internal policy question that had to be resolved in order to update the 1972 Common Program. In the spring of 1975 the FCP made public a *Charter of Civil Liberties*, which it favors as the preamble to a new constitution. Some of the articles in this document are quite interesting in and of themselves because they attempt to put into legislative form responses to many of the problems that affect contemporary society: violation of privacy, government-controlled data banks on private citizens, anti-Semitism, racism, prisons, preventive detention, freedom of residence, the death penalty, treatment of migrant workers, and so on.

The FCP is pursuing a double tactical objective: It wants to show that it is the leading exponent of civil liberties in France, and it wants to affirm that French democracy can be improved. But by reason of its internal logic, the subject shifts from the level of internal policy to the level of doctrine. How could it be otherwise when there have been so many opportunities since December 1975 at which the party expressed its disapproval of the "affairs" that rock the socialist world?

Before that date, however, the party was rather mute on these questions. In the sixties it became briefly involved only over the Siniavsky-Daniel trial. It criticized only one Soviet error—the publication of anti-Semitic tracts in the Ukraine. And it still acquiesced when the Soviet Union demanded the suppression of *Lettres françaises* after Aragon described normalization in Czechoslovakia as "a Biafra of the mind."

It continued obstinately to maintain right into 1974 that "Western democracy has nothing to teach the socialist regimes," and when Solzhenitsyn was threatened with banishment the best the party could do was to organize a meeting of Western European Communist parties in Geneva on "the extremely serious situation of intellectuals in capitalist countries." When Solzhenitsyn was exiled the next month (February 1974), the party merely expressed regret that only administrative sanctions had been taken against the writer, and at the same time it delivered an unusually perfidious personal attack against him.

It was necessary then to wait until December 1975 and the chance showing on French television of a BBC film about a labor camp in the Soviet Union for a bitter exchange to begin between Paris and Moscow. The first step was the hardest; the Pliouchtch affair, the mathematicians affair, the Wolff Biermann affair in East Germany, the *Aveu* affair, the Bukovsky-Corvalán affair, the Jewish culture symposium affair in Moscow, and the Charter 77 affair in Prague all provoked the FCP into increasingly vigorous objections.

From then on the ambivalence of the subject became evident. This is a subject that reflects what has been done by the established socialist system. It is thus forcing the FCP into a path that runs counter to the path chosen by the Soviet Union. Indeed, how is it possible to speak credibly about the attachment of Communists to basic rights, such as the right to strike, or about their hostility to such abuses as arbitrary internment in psychiatric institutions, arbitrary withdrawal of citizenship, granting of special privileges to those who belong to the party in power, and jurisdictional abuse between what is the state's and what is the party's, when it is evident that these rights do not exist in the socialist world, and that these abuses are the rule rather than the exception? And here is the most bizarre part: The persons who have been given the responsibility of making clear the French Communists' commitment to these rights, even in the Soviet Union, are precisely those men—Jean Kanapa, Francis Cohen, and Yves Moreau—who since 1956 have been responsible for affirming the contrary.

But perhaps this is not really an example of the bad faith of the Communist party as such, but, rather, is the application of an old Stalinist rule whereby those that should keep quiet the most are the ones made to do the talking.

Moreover, this is a subject that is vulnerable to exaggeration. Is the situation of civil rights and freedom in the France of Giscard d'Estaing the worst possible? We would be led to believe it: "They [Giscard's government] are frightened of everything that moves, thinks, imagines, and creates. Everywhere there are prohibitions, punishments, sanctions, blame, injustice, and arbitrariness. The media are under surveillance. Censorship and autocensorship are everywhere . . ." (Georges Marchais, *L'Humanité*, May 6, 1977). Are these exaggerations gratuitous? No, because they are intended to underscore the claim that the Communists can do better: "In the domain of freedom and democracy, and I can speak frankly, we are ready to compete with anyone, either now or in the future, because we do not fear anyone" (ibid.). To claim to do *better* is, with bombast and under the color of "expanding liberties," to be evasive about what is already done *well*.

The Italian Communist party, to be sure, which derives a major portion of its prestige and legitimacy from its struggle against fascism, appears both now and in the foreseeable future to want to maintain the Italian constitution, which was the common ground of the antifascist alliance after the war.

But what was the meaning of its campaign in 1976 to demand application of Article 40 of Reform Law 103 on the R.A.I., the Italian broadcast network, regarding limits on advertising broadcast in Italy by foreign television stations? Now that it has six of its members sitting with six Christian Democrats on the board of directors of the R.A.I. administration, the Italian Communist party plans to profit from its control over state television. Isn't it true that it wants to close down Télé-Monte-Carlo, which broadcasts daily the "Montanelli news review" (a program that follows the same political line as the Milan newspaper *Il Giornale nuovo*)?

As for the ambitions of the Spanish Communist party, it doesn't want anything more for the moment than to be able to participate legally in the kind of democracy that is developing in Spain. It did lose out, however, in its attempt to counter the political reforms supported by the king with the radical policy of "rupture" (although it was called "democratic rupture"), practiced from the summer of 1974 to the beginning of 1976 by the "democratic junta." The party was not even able to have this solution prevail against the more moderate program of the opposition sector known as the "Platform" group. The latter was able to get its program accepted by the "Democratic Coordination" group, made up of the junta and the "Platform" group. So the Communist party decided, in March 1976, to move from "democratic" rupture to "negotiated" rupture, a compromise that underscored the party's obligation to lower the stakes a bit. The stakes had to be lowered even more later, because the party then accepted as the Spanish flag the flag of the monarchy.

The French Communist party, whose constitutional legitimacy has never been challenged in the past thirty years, does not have to take such precautions. Therefore it is quite interesting to note that, under the heading of "expansion of basic liberties," the particular liberty that the party has given top priority to is "political freedom in the place of work"—in other words, the freedom for the Communist party to conduct its propaganda activities in places of employment. Its argument is that a worker does not stop being a citizen when he is in a factory; on the contrary, he is all the more a citizen at such times.

It is no less interesting to note that this demand is accompanied by a major campaign designed to convince the judiciary that this extension of rights does not require any modifications in existing legislation. According to the Communists, proper interpretation of the law would be sufficient to reach their goal:

> Even if the battle for political democracy in the place of work tends to give workers a new status there, in conformity with contemporary conditions in society, this battle does not necessarily imply a rupture with existing legislation; on the contrary, it simply requires that the law be applied to the fullest both in letter and in spirit (Roland Weyl, *France nouvelle*, September 6, 1976).

Before its reversal by the appeals court, the decision handed down by the Amiens court on August 10, 1976, against the Férodo Company had evoked sensational response. The company was sentenced to pay expenses for instigating the arrest of four Communist militants who had come into the factory to speak to workers. The court took up, almost word for word, the arguments made by the lawyer representing the Communist militants.

Now that we have reached the point where law, justice, the judiciary, and consequently the state are all involved, we have already reached the third area of debate: The abandonment of the concept of dictatorship of the proletariat.

On Wednesday January 7, 1976, *L'Humanité* published a letter in its Open Forum section, created to promote discussion of important topics before the Twenty-second Congress of the PCF (scheduled for February 4–8), from Georges Haddad, secretary of the Pablo Neruda cell in Epinay-sous-Sénart. Haddad proposed a new version of paragraph 9 of the preamble to the FCP statutes, suggesting that all reference there to the dictatorship of the proletariat be struck out. This deletion would be compensated by the addition of other wording in paragraph 11 to stress the role of the working class as the "directing force of the struggle for the transformation of society."

To support his proposal, Haddad developed four arguments. First, "dictatorship of the proletariat," although still having "basic and historical value," had applied only to "certain circumstances of the class struggle." Second, the various forms of fascism had given the term *dictatorship* a disastrous "resonance". Third, dictatorship would not really be compatible with the "ever larger concept of democracy that we are struggling for." And finally, "dictatorship of the proletariat" did not apply anymore, or, rather, it still applied, but it didn't "reflect the entire reality of today's world," especially in view of the changes that had taken place in the structure of the class struggle. The old "struggle of the working class and peasant proletariat," which had been the exclusive form of the class struggle for a long time, had been replaced "for the most part" by "the struggle of the working class in *alliance* with *broad* anti-monopolist support . . . within a large coalition around the working class, a decisive force . . . of a *union* of the French people."

That same evening, Georges Marchais was a guest on Antenna 2 television's "C'est-à-dire" ("Let's Make It Clear") program. Someone had obviously called the attention of the producer to a letter from an "unknown comrade," because he asked Marchais out of the blue what he thought of it. The Communist leader was obviously thinking of nothing else, for without a moment's hesitation he expressed his complete agreement with it and gave the very same reasons advanced by his party comrade: "Today the word *dictatorship* does not correspond with what we want. It has an unacceptable meaning that goes contrary to our goals and our basic theses." Marchais, whose passion for his work is well known, promptly furnished further evidence for the quite discouraging obsolescence into which Marxist terminology is being relegated these days: Not only is "the dictatorship of the proletariat" no longer acceptable, but "proletariat" itself is hardly any better. "The word *proletariat* is no longer suitable," he said, "because we want to join into the working class a majority of salaried workers as well."

It would be indecent to accuse French television of offering Georges

Marchais a forum merely for pouring old wine in new bottles. On the contrary, once again television itself created the event—and in the thorny area of philosophy.

After the first reactions in the press, notably that of Raymond Aron, in *Le Figaro* on January 12, who freely stated in the "Well, what next?" style that the question was important but needed clarification, Marchais twice spoke up again. The first occasion was at a press luncheon given on January 14 by the Central Committee in order to make it clear that the suppression of the term "dictatorship of the proletariat" was not just a semantic question, as some hostile commentators were implying. "It's not just a question of form," Marchais stated, "it's also a question of content." Then, on January 20, during the "Ten Questions and Ten Answers to Convince" program on France-Inter radio, Marchais repeated that "the dictatorship of the proletariat does not relate to the realities of our politics." Why not? Because "the force that will have the responsibility of carrying out the socialist transformation of society will be led by the working class, acting as the vanguard, but it will represent all the blue-collar and white-collar workers—the vast majority of today's French population." And what process would permit such vast representation? Universal suffrage: "At each step, we will both respect and see respected the people's choice freely decided by universal suffrage."

L'Humanité's Open Forum section went into gear right away, crisply, as befitted a well-broken-in machine. Nevertheless, this question was not raised in the initial text of the proposal, which had been the only document submitted for discussion to the cell assemblies, section conferences, and federation conferences being held in preparation for the Twenty-second Congress. The only thing one could know for sure was that the expression "dictatorship of the proletariat" was absent from the document, but several other expressions were also missing, and there was no reason to suspect that they had also been ostracized.

That must have been why it was necessary to wait five or six days, given the delays in the French postal system, for reactions to come in slowly to *L'Humanité*. After expressing support for the unexpected Haddad-Marchais proposal, these letters tried laboriously to play down the question. Some took an overly restrictive tack: "It would be impossible to consider joint rule with representatives of the big capitalists: the working class and its allies cannot and must not share power with the former exploiters once they have taken it," or "What really matters is the concrete content of Marxist-Leninist theory" (January 13). Others let their

dom of expression for all ideological and political opinions, an opposition press . . ." (January 15).

These exchanges of brief letters merely served as diversion while the
knights designated by the jousting headquarters sharpened their lances.
On one side it was Etienne Balibar, well known as an Althusser follower.
Since his side was designated in advance as the loser, this Quixote was
given the first chance to speak. On the next day—because it would not be
right to let people think for more than a few hours about the "wrong"
side of the question—Guy Besse took up the case on behalf of Georges
Marchais. Besse, an *agrégé* in philosophy and a member of the Politburo
of the party for fifteen years, could offer Marchais his political support
and his philosophical expertise.

After this exchange, the federation conferences unanimously approved the Marchais proposal. Having lived out its days still in harness
and covered with prestige, the dictatorship of the proletariat, less than
thirteen days after its fundamental inability to mean what it always had
meant had been publicly proclaimed, was sent into retirement, relegated,
in the words of an elementary-school teacher in the party, "to the history
books" after a listless debate, as Jean Kanapa admitted in the Communist
weekly, *France nouvelle*, on January 24. Although qualifying the discussion as "quite detailed, rich," he stated that "the party was nearly
unanimous in agreeing with the indictment of the necessity of the
dictatorship of the proletariat."

Should we attribute to stupor the silence that soon fell, after a brief
period of mourning, over the burial of the dictatorship of the proletariat
in the cemetery of forsaken "promised lands"? Yvonne Quiliès advanced
this hypothesis in *France nouvelle* on January 19, calling the stupor
unreasonable; it would have sufficed, she argued, to follow the path
taken by the party since the 1946 Maurice Thorez interview in the
London *Times* (exactly thirty years previously), the Champigny Manifesto (1968), and the *Défi Démocratique* [The Democratic Challenge] (1973)
in order to understand that the elimination of the dictatorship of the proletariat was nothing more than "a banal dot of the i." (Banal, the author
pointed out, in its "logical and not pejorative meaning.")

But the press clippings one was bound to collect for the cortege of a
veritable star of theory like the dictatorship of the proletariat reveal that
incredulity, rather than stupor, was the principal reaction to the event.
This was especially true of people who considered themselves close to the

Communists. In a poll of Communist voters taken by the IFOP [French Institute of Public Opinion] and the weekly magazine *Le Point* (in which the poll appeared on February 2, 1976), 54 percent of the respondents answered the question "Marchais proposes that his party abandon the 'dictatorship of the proletariat' concept. Does that better or worsen your opinion of the Communist party?" with "No change." During the next week, Jacques Ozouf made a rather witty comment upon another poll, taken of a general section of the public:

> The Communist leaders are like a group of frantic decorators who keep moving things around, empty the house, throw the icons in the garbage, push forward democracy, and pull backward the dictatorship of the proletariat, and through it all they aren't able to change the overall atmosphere (*Le Nouvel Observateur*, February 2, 1976).

The general reaction to this Communist initiative, even on the extreme Left (*Libération; Politique d'aujourd'hui*), which does not shirk from theoretical debate, even on abstract subjects, was ridicule. There was much more stifling of laughter than expression of indignation: Some thought that this decision was the dot over the i of the long-confirmed revisionism of the Communists; others found it in bad taste for the FCP to say anything about the dictatorship of the proletariat, which bore little relation, after the mauling it had received at the hands of the Stalinists, to the Marxist concept of the same name; while still others found that democratic credibility could not be bought with haphazard cosmetic changes.

Of course, the extreme left, as usual, was wrong. What was deserving of reproach in all this wasn't so much the stupor or skepticism but the incomprehension of it all because of ignorance. This ignorance reveals the hollowness of the assumption that thinking and working France since the 1960s has reached an advanced state of Marxization. On the contrary, and in line with what Daniel Lindenberg calls *Marxisme introuvable*, the serenity that greeted the proposal and execution of abolishing the dictatorship of the proletariat confirms what any study of the insurmountable obstacles encountered by Marxism in its attempt to penetrate French political or philosophical thought has given reason to suspect: People don't remember—if indeed they ever knew—that Engels considered the dictatorship of the proletariat, viewed as a part of the theory of the development of the capitalist mode of production, as one of the two great scientific discoveries of Marx (the other was the materialist concept of history). For Marx, as Maximilien Rubel has opportunely recalled, the dictatorship of the proletariat was not a political strategy made necessary by programmatic considerations, tactics, or circumstances: It was not capable of being changed at will. Rather, it was a necessary and inescapable period of transition in the evolution of society, a period that was utterly out of the control of human will.

The debate, therefore, was completely false in the manner it was presented to the public; it was artificial and poor, distorted, once theoretical analysis was not carefully distinguished from political analysis. Nevertheless, this debate had a certain sense; indeed, it had a proliferation of senses. It had sense in its immediate effects; it had sense in its uncertainty of sense; it had sense in what it unmasked, and in what it masked badly. What sense did it have in its effects? If everything seems to indicate that the FCP made the major decisions that pushed it into this new path in the fall of 1975, it was nevertheless the high-pitched ring of a cymbal one night on television that abruptly dismissed an abstract theoretical concept to the warehouse of discarded goods: That act constituted the unmistakable proclamation that a new era had begun. This was an example of inspired brutality destroying a delicate and sophisticated intellectual construction. Once again, what really counts is not having a doctrine but being able to violate it.

From this point, we reach the fourth debate, on pluralistic democracy. The acceptance by the FCP of such a democracy entails two important affirmations. First, there must be complete respect for universal suffrage, applied in its Western sense, of course. There would be no question of attempting—as the Portuguese revolutionary movement had in 1974—to substitute for the numerical electoral majority—the sole source of legality in bourgeois democracy—a pseudomajority based on "revolutionary legality."

The French Communists promise to respect universal suffrage not just during the initial period of participation as majority or minority parties in a Union of the Left government but for all time. They recognize that it would be possible, therefore, to lose by universal suffrage what they have gained by it; this is how the expression "alternating power" was coined. We might recall that this is a step Waldeck-Rochet could not dare to take. In his slow and cumbersome manner, compared with the free-wheeling style of Marchais, he saw that acceptance of "multipartyism" in the 1965–67 period would have been a first step away from Stalinism. Waldeck-Rochet, in effect, remained a prisoner of the scenario according to which the FCP would have to "defend" by all appropriate means, when it was threatened, the power that it had conquered. This was the only scenario that the Communists found acceptable. The memory of Lenin briskly disbanding the feeble Constituent Assembly in January 1918 was still prominent in the Communist imagination as the supreme act of the revolution in its glory. Perhaps it is in dealing with such subjects that we are most aware of how the deaths in the 1960s and the early 1970s of the "historical leaders"— Maurice Thorez, Jacques Duclos, and Benoît Frachon—have enabled the FCP to escape from the weight of its own legend.

Unlimited respect for universal suffrage is simply another way of saying that violence is no longer considered a method necessary for bringing about the new society, and this is the second affirmation that brings the FCP to pluralistic democracy.

But in this area as well the party has taken striking precautions to see that its concessions, which do go beyond the verbal level, do not overly constrain it. It has erected two protective railings in such a manner that the extent of its guarantees becomes somewhat doubtful.

First, the Communists rigidly maintain their conception of the economic structure upon which pluralistic democracy will rest: Nationalizations will reduce the private sector to a bare minimum. Here we can see the full meaning, which is more political than economic, of the Communist fight for nationalizations. The expansion to a near-monopoly level of the state's power of economic intervention—an expansion that threatens to be generalized and unrestricted—will compensate for adjustments made to fit in with political liberalism.

Next, the Communists also maintain a strict interpretation of their conception of the political instrument that will control the democratic process—the party itself. To be sure, the FCP has given up its claim to exercise the "guiding role" by substituting a less blunt formula— "guiding influence"—and the Spanish Communist party still states that it wants to function as a "guiding" force, not a "dominant" force. This search for the right word in no way diminishes the insistence with which it is recommended that the party be a *workers'* party, a *mass* party, one that has strong *roots* in *places of work*. Any discussion of the postrevolutionary state has only an uncertain meaning as long as the *party* that prefigures the *state* continues to project itself as a "new type of party," the Leninist party that carries a Leninist model of society.

How can it be any other way when the FCP works tirelessly to build up what it is that makes it original and assures it an exclusive and autonomous capability for political intervention: the hold of its leadership institutions over its grass-roots organizations; the existence of a well-established and diversified permanent apparatus; and finally its roots in the economic life of the country through its 8,000 cells in factories and places of work?

In a word, we can answer the question, "Has the FCP made a total commitment to respect the established democratic regime under any conditions?" with a blunt "No," because the party refuses to recognize democracy *as democracy*, insisting instead that it oppose its own democracy to the bourgeois pseudodemocracy: "The political leaders and spokesmen for the established bourgeoisie can babble all they want about human rights; the system they defend is exploitative and oppressive by its very nature. It is fundamentally hostile to democracy and to freedom." Or better yet, "Insofar as hostility to democracy is part of the very nature of modern capitalism, the fulfillment of freedom is needed for the development of socialism" (Georges Marchais, *L'Humanité*, May 6, 1977).

So all that we could concede under these conditions is that the FCP, on the eve of the day that it might be called upon to participate in government, has adjusted its own procedures to mesh with those of the established institutions without making any modifications in its continued judgment of these institutions.

4

A Regional Strategy?

who?

If it is not yet a variety of communism, is Eurocommunism a regional strategy for taking power?

First, a preliminary question: Is communism itself still a worldwide strategy for taking power? In other words, does the worldwide Communist movement still exist, or is it simply a myth? Ever since the abolition of the Communist International in 1943 and the abolition in turn of the Cominform—which was nothing more than a phantom institution—in 1956, what evidence is there, in the absence of stable, united, and centralized organizational structures possessing power and authority, that the worldwide Communist movement has any real consistency and coherence? World congresses meet somewhat irregularly; the last ones were held in 1960 and 1967. It would be problematic to convoke another one now that the Eurocommunist parties consider inappropriate even a pan-European conference similar to the one held in 1976, which the Soviets conceived of originally as the prelude to a subsequent world gathering. All that's left are "family reunions" made possible by the happy or sad events, planned or spontaneous, that constitute the fabric of world Communist sociability: funerals, anniversaries, celebrations, national congresses, et cetera.

But does this mean that the world Communist movement has irreversibly decomposed and split into autonomous parties? Have the concerns of these parties for their own interests displaced their concerns for the general interests of the group they reputedly belong to? Is Alexander Dallin correct when he observes, "In fact, it is difficult to think of a single attribute except the name that is shared by *all* Communist parties, and *only* by them"?

Stalin would no doubt be surprised by the trouble Brezhnev has in getting across to his supporters: Things were more expeditious in the "old days." But it would be a mistake to attribute Brezhnev's difficulties only to the inauspicious events. To be sure, the schism with China has been entirely negative, even though Peking has not been able to develop the drawing power of its rival, Moscow. By contrast, Tito's rebellion, besides facilitating the satellitization process of the other people's democracies and the Stalinization process of the Western European Communist parties, had neither grave nor irreversible consequences. And, most of all, a significant share of Brezhnev's problems is paradoxically due to the successes represented by the expansion of the world Communist movement in regions and areas where Stalin had not shown much talent; the entire Third World is likely now to supply new recruits, clients, and allies to the world Communist movement. Finally, many Communist parties before the war were more or less clandestine sects that were able to suvive only through the aid in men, money, arms, and literature supplied by the Comintern, unless they had simply retreated to winter quarters by finding a temporary hiding place in Moscow.

Many of these parties have been able, through various means—including identifying with ethnic concerns, caste and language considerations, peasant revolts, or military rebellions, or, most often, in the Western countries at least, by a slow process of adaption to their sociopolitical and cultural environments—to develop substance, a raison d'être, and legitimacy, which assured them the ability to grow and perpetuate themselves. Under these conditions, they now have a position to negotiate from and the self-confidence to move about as they choose.

The world Communist movement must deal with such varied and such inconsistent elements that it is easy to understand why it can rarely, and then only with great difficulty, speak with a single voice and in a self-assured manner; but this does not mean that it cannot speak at all.

While it is premature to label the world Communist movement as only a myth or even a simple abstraction, it would also be out of line to state that Eurocommunism has already crystallized into a regional strategy for taking power. Marchais has spoken clearly on this subject: "There is not now and there cannot be a return to a centralized system in the Communist movement of either world or regional dimensions" (*L'Humanité*, February 14, 1977).

To be sure, one could reason that the coaching role played by the Italian Communist party in the development of the French and Spanish parties argues in favor of a regional strategy. The quality of the relations carried on between the leaderships of the French and Italian parties might well constitute the best indicator of the uncertainties that have burdened the emergence of the Eurocommunist phenomenon. These relations were terrible until 1964 because of the age-old personal animosity between Thorez and Togliatti, which the diverging analyses of the 1956 events merely accentuated, but from 1964 to 1968 there was a first period of détente that corresponded to the first liberalization efforts carried out in the FCP under the direction of Waldeck-Rochet. Relations worsened once again from 1968 to 1973 because of differences between the parties regarding the Soviet normalization policies in Czechoslovakia and also because of the Soviet support given to Marchais's rise in the FCP. They seemed to improve in 1973–74, but worsened again in the following year because of the Portuguese situation, and did not improve again until the sensational turn of events in the fall of 1975.

And since that fall, to be sure, when almost simultaneously the FCP abandoned the astonished Soviets at the preparatory meeting for the pan-European conference, joined the "four musketeers" (Italy, Spain, Romania, and Yugoslavia), and then went to Rome—like making a trip to Canossa—turning the visit into a "historic" voyage, the rapprochement of the Italian and French Communist parties and the warm ties between the Italian and Spanish Communist parties has led the three parties to converging analyses and behavior.

But there is still quite some distance between these developments and a regional strategy.

A step in this direction was no doubt taken when a Madrid "summit" brought together the three leaders of the only parties that accept the Eurocommunist label: Berlinguer, Carrillo, and Marchais. Until the beginning of 1977, they had taken care to keep their relations on the bilateral level, which had been considered legitimate since 1956: the Italian-Spanish meeting at Leghorn in July 1975, the Franco-Italian meeting at Rome in November 1975 and at Paris in June 1976, and the Italian-Spanish conference at Rome in September 1976.

But once the trilateral-meeting stage had been reached, the Eurocommunist leaders did not want to or were not able to go beyond it. On one hand, they have always maintained that their Madrid conference was technically a meeting of solidarity between the Italian and French parties to show support for the Spanish Communist party's struggle for legalization—this was a more acceptable format for Moscow. Moreover, it is not certain that the "interference" of foreign Communist parties in Spanish affairs has been entirely beneficial for Carrillo. On the other hand, they limited themselves to a somewhat dull joint communiqué that would require abundant goodwill to be seen as the birth certificate of Eurocommunism, which had not yet even been baptized. Finally, Georges Marchais took on the task of explaining why the three parties had made no specific reference to the Soviet dissidents: "We consider that three Communist parties meeting together do not have the right to make a collective judgment condemning any party." He then pointed reprovingly to the unfortunate earlier examples of the excommunications of Tito and Mao. There was no reason, anyway, to excommunicate Brezhnev—merely to ask him to explain certain aspects of his politics. But what was the good of meeting as a threesome and then saying nothing about the important subjects at hand?

The three parties would have to share a common political line, if not a common style, in order for us to find that there is a unified regional strategy, not a discontinuous series of agreements on varying levels of importance. But what do we really find? The three parties always divide two-against-one in each of three possible configurations.

First configuration: the French and Italian Communist parties on one side and the Spanish on the other. This configuration becomes apparent as soon as one looks at the internal situations of the parties and of the world Communist movement. Does the Spanish Communist party feel itself more open than the other parties to manipulations by the Soviet party, which has no scruples when dealing with a small party caught in hopeless opposition against a firmly rooted power? Before coming down hard against Carrillo at last in June 1977 (we will come back to this subject later), the Soviet party had already publicly criticized Manuel Azcarate, who is in charge of the foreign policy section of the SCP, and had twice supported unsuccessful internal coups designed to oust Carrillo. The only defense available to the Spanish party was to keep its distance from the "big brother in the East." In seven years Carrillo ventured to Moscow only twice.

Or would it be more accurate to say that the Spanish Communist party is in the process of sending out roots and rebuilding itself and that consequently its structure and actions are less formed and more flexible than those of the other two parties, one of which, the French, is nearly sixty years old, while the Italian is over thirty?

Or should we conclude instead that Santiago Carrillo is in essence more daring than his two colleagues—on democratic centralism, for example? This is what Carrillo himself implied when he said on French television on July 13, 1977, "I'm guided by theoretical considerations; I want Eurocommunism to be Marxist. . . ."

Second configuration: the Italian and Spanish parties on one side and the French on the other. On almost all foreign policy issues where the three parties do not line up in unison with Soviet policy, the Italian and Spanish parties appear to disagree profoundly with the FCP.

The Italian Communist party accepts the fact that détente implies an American-Soviet bipolar understanding. As Pierre Hassner has pointed out, this condominium would be equivalent on a worldwide scale to the historic compromise on the Italian scale. Although its hostility to the initial premise that led to the creation of NATO has not abated, since 1969 the ICP has progressively refrained from considering it as an exclusively aggressive institution. It now sees NATO as a force contributing to equilibrium, as long as the disbanding of military coalitions in Europe has not been put on the agenda. The Italian Communist party must take into account the strategic situation of Italy: if the Warsaw Pact bloc should absorb Yugoslavia after the death of Tito, then the Soviet army would be on the eastern frontier of Italy. It is difficult under these conditions to persuade the public that Italy should leave NATO. The Italian Communist party would be satisfied, then, without specifying the details, with a "revision and restructuring of the alliance." It would even be difficult to insist upon the dismantling of American bases in Italy. Berlinguer took one further step when he admitted during the 1976 election campaign that it is only in the shadow of the Atlantic Alliance that the Italian Socialist experience can be spared the fate of the Prague Spring.

The ICP also gives considerable importance to the European unification issue. It refuses to treat the question as one of camouflaged German resurgence, preferring instead to consider European unification as the essential terrain of its own *aggiornamento* and the linchpin of its alliances within the European Communist movement. This is the basis on which it has negotiated with the Spanish Communist party since 1969. In a courteous but polemical exchange with Jean-Paul Sartre in March 1977, which escalated bizarrely on the subjects of the French Communist party's anti-Atlanticism and anti-Germanism, Alberto Jacoviello

presented the ICP's position on the unification of Europe. A refusal to
consider the creation of a unified Europe, he argued, under the pretext
that such a Europe "would bear no relationship to the 'workers' Europe'
that the Western workers movement has dreamed of for a century"
(Sartre, *Le Monde*, February 10, 1977), would indicate "profound skepticism on the role of the workers movement and of the Left in general, and
would cast both the movement and the Left into subordinate positions or,
at best, into an eternal wait for the 'historic occasion.'" Jacoviello further
elaborated, "To be sure, and Sartre is right on this, our number one
target today should be the drift toward German-American domination
in Western Europe, but we must not lose sight of two elements; first, the
German-American leadership is neither a given factor nor an unchangeable element; second, history does not wait around for those who are
absent, especially when their efforts might change its course."

For its part, the Spanish Communist party is more suspicious than the
Italian party of the benefits that might come from an eventual reciprocal neutralization of the two major powers. In an interview given to
Manifesto [Turin] on November 1, 1975, Santiago Carrillo considered
that the coming to power of the Left in Europe might constitute a source
of tension with both the United States and the Soviet Union; the latter,
according to him, fears competition from a new model of socialism.
Profiting from the fact that Spain is not a member of the unified military
command in NATO, Carrillo would prefer to play the nonalignment
card, in the manner of Yugoslavia or North Korea. Even though he no
longer expressly asks for the closure of American bases in Spain, he has
assumed a kind of Gaullist-Communist position.

But the Spanish Communist party is no less pro-European than the
ICP, and perhaps for the same reason that Giorgio Amendola advanced
to explain the attachment of Italian Communists to the European
Economic Community: "Italians have been obliged to emigrate. We have
millions of Italians in France, Germany, Belgium, Switzerland, etc., who
because of the EEC are already able to benefit from new rights." We
might recall on this subject the blowup between Georges Marchais and
Santiago Carrillo during the conference of Common Market Communist parties in January 1974. It was on the very subject of the treatment
of migrant workers.

By contrast, the French Communist party considers itself a "good
European" only on the condition that Europe become a "real Europe," a
Europe that requires no surrender of sovereignty and is freed from the

double hegemony of America and Germany. To be sure, it has already been pointed out that the FCP, in order not to cause serious tension with its two best allies inside and outside of France—the French Socialist party and the Italian Communist party—agreed not to wage the kind of loud and effective campaign brought to bear against the European Defense Community in 1954.

And furthermore, after reaffirming for months that he would condemn in the strongest possible terms the election of the European parliament by universal suffrage, Georges Marchais stated abruptly, on April 17, 1977, with no more advance notice than that given for the abandonment of the dictatorship of the proletariat concept, and by a similar use of the media: "The election of the national delegation for the European parliament by universal suffrage raises no problems for us. . . . It is effectively a democratic process." Questioned earlier, Marchais had said, "If eventually *the election law were to contain a binding and solemn engagement for the persons elected,* forbidding them *under any circumstances* from questioning national independence and sovereignty— in other words, if the prerogatives of the French National Assembly and the Constitution of the French Republic were to be guaranteed—then we could examine the question" (*L'Humanité's* italics).

In short, the FCP was henceforth prepared to accept the election by universal suffrage of the French representatives to the European Assembly. The party would do this, first, because it was in accordance with the Treaty of Rome, and the Communists, once they had recognized the "reality" of the EEC (Brezhnev did so explicitly in 1972), also accepted article 138; but also because the election of French representatives to the European Assembly by universal suffrage would be carried out by proportional representation in 1978 on the national level, which assures the Communists of the proper representation. By contrast, the FCP remains hostile to any increase of the powers of the European Assembly at the expense of national parliaments.

Has Marchais thus become a "European" in the manner of Berlinguer? Some observers hope so; others have pointed out that he just wants to have a more flexible formula than Berlinguer, to allow him to demonstrate his goodwill vis-à-vis his Socialist allies without at the same time relinquishing to the Gaullists the monopoly on the fight for national independence. This new formulation has just enough ambiguity to serve alternatively in both senses. After all, if the FCP supports a reinforcement at the European level of the power of parliament (where it will have some influence through the Communist group) at the expense of the executive power of the Commission and the Council of Ministers (where it has no influence), it is by contrast opposed to any transfer of power from the French parliament (where it has a relative position of strength) to the European parliament (where, even with the support of the Italians, the Communist group is and will be in a position of relative weakness vis-à-vis the Christian Democratic, Liberal, and especially the Social-Democratic groups).

Third configuration: the Italian Communist party on one side and the French and Spanish parties on the other. This is the way the parties line up in the realm of domestic politics. The Italian Communist party adopted an internal strategy based on its nonparticipatory support of the minority and monolithic Christian Democratic government; the party consequently approves in general principle, if not in all of its applications, the austerity policy that all Western European governments have invoked to "manage the crisis." Enrico Berlinguer has even gone so far as to sketch out how such a policy could open the way for a definition of a new type of society that would avoid the pitfalls of the society of consumerism and would be based, rather, on another system of values, including the value of poverty. Should we see in this inclination of the Italian party's general secretary a resurgence of the Franciscan notions appropriate to Italian Catholicism? Is it more like the harsher dissidence of a Savonarola? Can we see in it the echo of a Protestantism that the Counter-Reformation hunted down, of which the Italian Communist party might be a final lay practitioner in the visionary style of the Socinians of Poland? Or is it only a consequence of aristocratic boredom with the endless race toward the accumulation of goods?

The French and Spanish Communist leaders, by contrast, perhaps because they are themselves from more humble origins and have firsthand knowledge of what poverty is, and do not find it to be quaint and charming, hold steadfastly to the idea that it is not for them to preach the virtues of a life of privation to the workers, but rather to rally them to the struggle against paying for the consequences of the crisis.

In fact, if the three Eurocommunist parties are in disagreement, it is because their respective internal strategies belong to two different epochs in the history of the world Communist movement. That of the Union of the Left belongs to the already classic era opened in the mid-1930s with alliances of the United Front, Popular Front, and National

Front type. After 1968, the FCP realized that Gaullist power was nearing its end. Because of the "positive" aspects of de Gaulle's foreign policy, the party had been a pole of opposition without ever being likely to become an alternative to power, but after de Gaulle the party chose to return more directly to a Frontist policy of leftist union, signifying that it considered the united opposition, by winning the elections, might become an alternative and achieve power. The substitution in 1974 of the Giscardian government for the Gaullist legacy shifted the pole of opposition from the Communist party to the Socialist party and could only accentuate the determination of the Communists to opt for the Union of the Left. It was for this reason, moreover, and we shall return to the subject later, that the party felt it necessary to devalue the "positive aspects" of French foreign policy and deprive Giscard of the license that had been accorded to Gaullism.

The historical compromise in the Italian manner belongs to a more recent period that began in the 1960s. The tardiness of the FCP in beginning de-Stalinization with as much determination as the ICP made it miss this innovation; the FCP could henceforth adopt it only after the present tactic of the Union of the Left has run its course.

There are indeed considerable differences between these two approaches. Most important is that one approach makes it absolutely necessary to assure the survival as a force in national politics of the Socialist party, which would be a partner in a common program, at the risk that the Socialists would abuse the program for their purposes; in the other approach, this precaution is not as important. This explains the difference in the desire for change and renovation between the Italian and the French Communist parties. Because the Italian Communist party constitutes the "entire Left," it has to adjust its own image in keeping with its broad functions; because the French Communist party, on the other hand, is only the Communist component of the Union of the Left, it is freer to maintain its own image. It is only the image of the leftist union that it must protect, to be sure that this image does not lose its appeal.

It is clear why a regional strategy cannot crystallize: once the grasp of the world Communist system over each national party weakens, these parties fall not into a regional Communist system but into the control of the national political systems in which each party is rooted. Michel Roccard has analyzed this quite well: "From the moment when each national Communist party decides to give the matters of its own country top priority, well, the Italian situation, the French situation, and the Spanish situation are so different that there is no common element shared by them all."

The result, therefore, is "Socialism under the colors of France," which has much less to do with Eurocommunism than with national communism—several none-too-happy examples of which we have already seen during the history of the Communist phenomenon—which I would be tempted to label "communism in the Romanian style."

5

The Temptation of National Communism?

Now we have reached the threshold of the third possible definition of Eurocommunism—the temptation, shared by the three parties, of national communism. What does this temptation include? It does not necessarily mean the casting off of the lines that moor each Communist party to the world Communist movement, nor even the increasing of the distance within this movement between the center and the periphery. It is, instead, the temptation to review and lighten the sum total of the obligations called *proletarian internationalism* inherent in each Communist party by virtue of the priority it gives to its membership in the world Communist movement.

What, for example, does the French Communist party mean when it proposes to establish "socialism under the colors of France"?—a felicitous slogan, we might add. Does this mean that socialism has universal validity but that it best corresponds to local needs when repainted in the hues of France? Or is it rather a question of making a prototype whose structure and function are designed specifically for France? If this is the case, then what are the special French characteristics that should influence this original socialism? What is there in the Communist program—as it is found in the pamphlet *Changing Course*—that is particularly French? Or, to look at the problem from another angle, how could a socialist regime, once it is firmly rooted in France, not be "French"? We can understand that the political culture of a given country, depending on its original degree of receptivity to socialism in its Bolshevik form, provides varying opportunities for socialism to adhere to the political and social body; and we can also understand that the political culture would favor a variety of socialism that, by reason of its application of socialist principles, could be called closer to or farther from the initial socialist model. But the question of degree, the adverbial modifiers, is only of secondary importance: daily life might be more difficult, or it might be more pleasant, but life itself is not affected. It is certainly nicer to live in Budapest than in Moscow, but the logic of life itself is the same in both places.

So we might well wonder whether the proposal of "socialism under the colors of France" does not stem from a more simple objective. What is especially French is not so much the thing itself as the scale on which the project is to be realized. This will be a new version of a well-established theme, the French path to a kind of socialism that has no particular specific national traits other than those incidental to any ordinary historical phenomenon.

What is socialism on the French scale? During the Third International (1919–43), the FCP considered itself nothing more than an organized wing of the great revolutionary proletarian army, whose general staff, the Executive Committee of the Comintern, was in Moscow. From 1943 through 1976, through different institutional arrangements, the FCP considered itself a component of the world Communist system. Does it view itself today as an autonomous and isolated entity? We would be tempted to think so after hearing Georges Marchais affirm, on June 23, 1977, "We have definitely left any international organization." They have left an organization that, to be sure, no longer exists. But are they free from the obligations that come from belonging to the world Communist movement, to the Socialist camp? This movement and camp are realities that cannot, perhaps, be called *organizations*, but they are realities nevertheless.

To find out where things stand we should examine the FCP's attitudes toward proletarian internationalism and its practical implications.

The traditional version of proletarian internationalism has characteristics that fall under three headings:

1. Reliance upon the universality of the Soviet socialist model in both its parts: as a model for taking power and as a model for the establishment of socialism after the takeover;
2. Accordance of a high priority to the obligations of and the advantages inherent in membership in the world Communist movement, which requires that the national strategy of each party must orient

itself and adjust itself to the overall strategy of the world movement;

3. Defense of the foreign policy establishing the community of socialist states, the interstate part of the world Communist movement.

While not contesting the continued legitimacy of these characteristics, the Eurocommunist parties would prefer that the confusion they themselves helped to sow between "Communism" and "Sovietism" be less constraining. They want to keep socialism a worthy and dignified system, to prevent it from losing its reputation in history. It is on this basis that the Eurocommunist parties make the following demands: to be allowed to criticize questionable aspects of Soviet actions; to challenge the centrality of the Soviet Union and its primacy, in fact and in right, over the other components of the world Communist movement, by favoring an international movement with several centers (the Italian polycentrist thesis) or by affirming that there is no center at all (the French position); finally, to be allowed to air out the foreign policy of socialist states in order to be able to keep some room for maneuvering on those questions closest to their own national interests.

In practical terms, how far along is the work of reshaping proletarian internationalism? In fact, not very far along.

Under the first heading, which concerns the model furnished by socialist countries to world socialist development, it is true that we frequently hear criticism from the Eurocommunist parties, and this is certainly a new development. But these parties did not originate this criticism: playing the role of the Greek chorus at best, the Communist parties have not taken the initiative in denouncing either past or present types of action or specific unacceptable actions, even though they have been in better positions than most to know these abuses, because they have even been the victims of them in the past. Moreover, the criticisms that the Communist parties articulate concern violations of human rights "when there have been *slurs* against freedom, *inadequacy* in the democratic nature of life in countries that *nevertheless* have inaugurated socialism" (Marchais, May 6, 1977). Slurs? Inadequacy? The terminology is benign.

The FCP remains vague about the general applicability of the Soviet economic and political model in the West: it is one thing to say that it will act in its own way and will do better, if possible; it is something else to eliminate from future consideration the major characteristics of the Soviet experience, such as central planning and administrative price setting. The FCP is also not ready to recognize the persistent mediocrity of the Soviet economic performance, at least in those sectors that are of greatest interest to civil society. It continues to cite initial backwardness and capitalist encirclement as reasons for the recurring weakness of the economy; and it continues to put full blame on the climate for the shaky agricultural situation.

Berlinguer took a similar approach in his preparatory report to the Central Committee for the Fourteenth Congress in 1974: "In spite of everything, the creation of a new infrastructure based on the state's ownership of the means of production and on the abolition of the old ruling classes, as well as reference to the Marxist principles of the liberation of man, has, in spite of acute initial retardation, allowed the development of the economy, of good social conditions, and of a civil and moral atmosphere better in these key respects than what can be found in the West." Again, both at Bucharest during his visit to President Ceauşescu and during his Milan speech in February 1977, he spoke of the "irreversibility of socialism in the East" and of the "superiority of socialist production relations."

At a Madrid press conference in March 1977, when Marchais, Berlinguer, and Carrillo were peppered with questions about the "democratic and socialist superstructure in the USSR," all three hesitated and waffled on the question. Marchais maintained that there was "a certain socialist democracy" there; Berlinguer stated that there was no more exploitation of one man by another and, as K. S. Karol reported, that "the important decisions in internal and international politics there are made in the interests of the manual laborers, peasants, and other workers." Santiago Carrillo, finally, explained that he "had been misunderstood when he spoke of the domination of one social group over the rest of Soviet society."

More significant yet is the ritual approval that the FCP continues to provide for the procedures of "building socialism" in the most recently conquered countries: Vietnam, Angola, and even Cambodia. It was in this vein that the party recently communicated, without reticence, it would seem, some disturbing information about "the redeployment of manpower in Vietnam" and gave publicity to the statement by Pham Van

Dong that "rehabilitation centers are really an expression of the principle of respect for human rights, if one understands what this concept
means" (*L'Humanité*, April 23, 1977).

Under the second heading—membership of the world Communist
movement—the FCP has always been careful to maintain close relations
with other Communist parties and to coordinate policies with them. The
volume of diplomatic contacts undertaken by the very active foreign
policy section of the Central Committee has in no way diminished; on the
contrary, as indicated by the frequency of French Communist missions
to foreign Communist parties and the reciprocal reception of foreign
Communist delegations in France, it has remained substantial, if for
nothing more than such periodic events as the party's national congress
every two years or for the annual *L'Humanité* gathering. In September
1976, forty-nine foreign delegations came to Paris for this latter event.
They represented fourteen socialist countries, including the Soviet
Union; the principal countries of Western Europe; and Japan, South
Africa, Australia, Latin America, Africa (Somalia and the Polisario
Front), and the Middle East (Iraq, Iran, and Oman). Last year, delegations from the Lebanese Communist party and the PLO were particularly honored:

> The dominant note, a symbol of a very special sympathy and solidarity,
> was signaled by thousands of scarves dappled pink or gray, the colors
> of the Palestinian fighters, half-covering the faces in the crowd. Lebanese
> and Palestinian martyrs of Tall al Zaatar, your sacrifices have not been in
> vain, because at such a great distance we pay your cause the most fervent
> homage (*L'Humanité*, September 13, 1976).

The only change has been the dramatic drop in contacts between the
FCP and the Soviet Communist party. Since 1975 Marchais has not met
with Brezhnev, Suslov, Ponomarev, or Zagladin, in spite of the many
opportunities furnished in 1976 by the Twenty-second FCP Congress in
Paris, the Twenty-fifth Congress of the Soviet Communist Party in
Moscow, and the Conference of European Communist Parties in East
Berlin. (It was in Berlin that Brezhnev took the time to meet not only
with Berlinguer and Cunhal but also with the lesser-known leaders of
such diminutive Communist parties as those of Great Britain and West
Germany.) According to Vasil Bil'ák, Marchais refused to meet with

Chervonenko, the Soviet ambassador in Paris, at the beginning of 1977, when he requested an interview to explain to the French leader the Soviet party's point of view. And when Brezhnev came to Paris in person to confer with President Giscard d'Estaing in June 1977, there were no private meetings, unlike earlier visits, in the embassy salons between the Soviet and French general secretaries. There were indeed a few study groups from the FCP that visited the Soviet Union in 1976, as well as Soviet visits to France, but these were merely routine visits and their objectives were of secondary importance. One visit was to observe the work of propaganda and education departments, while another was to study the treatment of municipal, regional, and urban questions. And even when such important Soviet dignitaries as Ponomarev, Inozemtsev, and Zhukov came to Paris in December 1976 for a disarmament conference, they were welcomed only by two second-level FCP representatives.

What is at stake here, for the moment anyway, is less the principles of international communism than the relative place within this international activity of bilateral relations between the FCP and the Soviet Communist party.

The evolution of these relations is comparable to the evolution of relations between the Japanese Communist party and its Soviet counterpart. Under the chairmanship of Miyamoto Kenji, the Japanese party has followed since 1961 a "naturalization" process designed to make it an important force in national politics. On one hand, the Japanese party has asserted its right to a policy of independence that would be "established only in Tokyo" (July 18, 1976). Since 1963, when it refused to endorse the temporary partial test ban treaty signed by the Soviet Union, the Japanese Communist party has been involved in several tumultuous confrontations with both the Soviet and the Chinese Communist parties (1963, 1966, 1974). The many efforts on both sides to bring about a normalization, such as the Miyamoto-Suslov meeting in Tokyo in 1968 and the Miyamoto-Brezhnev meeting in Moscow in 1971, have not really been successful, although there was a sign of warmer relations in 1976 when the Soviet ambassador to Tokyo visited the JCP's Central Committee. In July 1977 the JCP did cross a Rubicon of sorts by publishing an indictment in its organ *Akahata* (Red Flag) against "the stance taken by the USSR as a major interventionist power" on the Kuriles question. *Pravda*, in its June 12, 1977, issue, had pointed out that this was probably the first time, publicly and in violation of the principles of Marxism-Leninism, that a "frontier problem" had been "the object of a dispute between Communist parties."

On the other hand, the JCP has compensated for this trend and sought to avoid isolation by developing close relations and ties of friendship with several Communist parties in Southeast Asia and Western Europe, especially those of Vietnam, France, Italy, and Spain. Since 1967 there have been four exchanges of delegations between the Japanese and the French parties—1967, 1971, 1973, and 1976.

We find here the propensity of the FCP—shared by the JCP—to put more emphasis in its New Look on the nationalist component than the Italian Communist party does. The ICP, whose responsibility for the rise of Eurocommunist ideas and tendencies is earlier than that of the French party, has kept its relations with the Soviet Communist party on an apparently friendly basis. Berlinguer personally attends congresses in the Soviet Union, as has been the tradition for the past fifty years for general secretaries of large parties. He sent his regards on the occasion of Brezhnev's seventieth birthday, and he warmly receives Soviet visitors in Rome. In return, the Soviet ambassador in Rome continues to show great consideration for Italian Communist delegations at his receptions, while exhibiting a cold but correct attitude toward official representatives of the Italian government. In short, the ICP is careful to make clear that its disagreements with the Soviet Communist party concern only certain aspects of the internal politics of the international Communist movement. It is well known that the ICP deplores the sharpness of the Sino-Soviet dispute and wants to offer its good offices to reconcile these two enemy brother-states. In the Czechoslovak affair, it emphasized less the question of the *sovereignty* of the Czechoslovak state, albeit a socialist state, than the desirability of finding some means other than armed force to resolve intrasocialist conflicts.

Moreover, at the pan-European conference in June 1976, Brezhnev was willing to accept in substitution for the term *proletarian internationalism* an updated version that was free of the burden of the past and of bad memories—*internationalist solidarity*. This was a verbal concession that may, like any similar concession, either fall into disuse or develop into something more substantial.

In the short run, the most important function of "internationalist solidarity" seems to be to prevent the Eurocommunist parties from becoming too concerned, other than "demagogically" (to use Vadim

Delaunay's expression), with the plight of dissidents in the socialist world. As Branko Lazitch has observed (*Le Point*, February 21, 1977), while a member of the Italian Central Committee, Professor Lombardo Radice, states that it was "inevitable that *socialist* opposition to the Eastern governments link up, at least ideologically, with Eurocommunism," André Amalrik has remained lucidly skeptical. In Rome in October 1976 Amalrik, addressing the Italian Communists, shouted bitterly, "We Soviet dissidents have always held out our hands to you, but you have preferred to shake those of our oppressors!" Amalrik's criticism was only confirmed by the regrettable crudeness with which *L'Humanité*, on July 19, 1977, called President Carter's concern for the defense of human rights a "humanitarian pretense."

Berlinguer's ostentatious reception of Alvaro Cunhal and Luis Corvalán shows that, after being put off briefly by the aggressive pro-Soviet stance of the Portuguese and the Chilean, he did not want to make too big a deal out of it, which is another way of saying that the dissidents in the East are wrong to make such a big deal out of their situation.

Such Eurocommunist *Realpolitik* is inevitable once the Communist leaders decide in a general way to make the most of the advantages that accrue to them from membership in a worldwide movement. The French Communists, as well as the others, never tire of stating that the chances for social change in France increase in relation to changes tending to favor socialism on the world level:

> We are proposing to our people the democratic and revolutionary path to socialism, taking into account the conditions of our era and our country as well as the array of basic conditions that has been considerably modified in favor of the forces of progress, freedom, and peace (Georges Marchais, *L'Humanité*, January 20, 1977).

Here is the crux of the question: Eurocommunists make no change in their vision of world communism. They continue to see the world as divided in two camps bearing the well-established labels, respectively, of nefarious imperialism and of marvelous socialism.

Since reorganizing itself in 1955, the Japanese Communist party, for example, has worked out a policy in a particularly careful, rigorous, and, when necessary, abrupt manner that seeks—even to the point of a public and explicit rupture of relations—to reject any Soviet or Chinese tutelage. This is what it calls its "true patriotism" policy. It has, nevertheless, in its foreign policy position made a central point of its fight against American imperialism—what it calls its practice of "true pro-letarian internationalism."

Consequently it is not surprising that the Eurocommunist parties cannot break away more completely from the Soviet Union. At the most they might insist that the Soviet Communist party get back in line with the world Communist movement—considered as a group of equal parties; but they cannot deny to the Soviet state its leadership of the anti-imperialist camp in the international arena without depriving it of what makes up its force and its power. At the most they might stress to an unreasonable degree a radical orientation toward the Third World in order to link up directly with the national and colonial liberation move-ment; but when things become serious, as in Angola, Zaïre, and the Middle East, it is necessary to rely upon Soviet tutelage. Finally, they might at the most be critical of Soviet treatment of its dissidents; but when the dissidents threaten not to "bring back the Cold War," but to cast confusion on the essential and the only real line of demarcation, the separation between the two worlds, the two "camps," then things fall apart.

The "struggle against fascism" made it impossible during the 1930s to denounce the Stalinist massacres. The "struggle for détente" does not make it impossible to carry out the struggle for freedom today: that in itself constitutes progress. But these two battles must be carried on simultaneously. "I think that it would be dangerous," Georges Marchais said on February 22, 1977, "to pit the struggle for freedom and the struggle for détente and peaceful coexistence against each other. We must not return to the politics of the Cold War, and we must do every-thing to prevent war. So the two battles should be waged together. I must say that insofar as the problems relating to peaceful coexistence and international détente are concerned, we see nothing to reproach Soviet policy for." This is what Berlinguer said to the London *Times*, nearly word for word, in February 1976:

We support the fundamental philosophy behind the policy of peaceful coexistence that is being practiced by the Soviet Union. But we do not see why this should occasion surprise. It would be irresponsible for us not to recognize what is widely recognized elsewhere, that the Soviet Union's peace is in the general interest of mankind.

It thus follows that under the third heading—supporting the foreign policy of the socialist camp—the old practices have been strictly adhered to. One sign of this is the priority, or at least the relatively important spot, compared with what other political families do, accorded to foreign policy concerns by the socialist camp. Another is the general report on foreign policy made by Jean Kanapa to the FCP Central Committee on June 23, 1976. But, above all, in scrutinizing the nearly daily concrete policy positions taken on Atlanticism, Germany, national defense, disarmament, Franco-Soviet economic cooperation, Vietnam, Korea, Berlin, Lebanon and the Middle East, the Sahara, Djibouti, the Comoro Islands, Angola, Rhodesia, South Africa, Zaïre, French Africa, the French overseas departments and territories, and Latin America, it is impossible to find any spot on the globe where the policy supported by the FCP, reputedly a "truly French" policy, differs in its analysis, conclusions, and proposals from Soviet policy.

There is but a single point of serious disagreement, which comes, in fact, from internal policy in France: the degree of sacrifice that can be asked of a single Communist party in the name of the general interest of the entire Communist movement, such as is understood and interpreted by the policies of the Soviet Union.

The French Communists dispute the legitimacy of extending to President Giscard d'Estaing the benefit of being considered exceptional, which had been accorded to General de Gaulle by virtue of the "positive aspects" of his foreign policy and to President Pompidou as the direct, and respectful, heir to the Gaullist legacy. They consider it unfair to deprive the leftist opposition of whatever greater opportunities might befall it from a less divided Soviet sympathy, considering that the foreign policy of President Giscard, an indirect heir who is for the most part unfaithful to his legacy, cannot maintain many of the "positive aspects" of Gaullist policy. The French Communists are in effect more vigilant and more punctilious than the "historic Gaullists," watching for the least deviation from the diplomatic traditions of General de Gaulle, and they view these traditions as unchangeable positions of principle. They hope to be able to convince the Soviets of the correctness of their thesis: that the major interests of the Soviet state are not at stake to the point where the interests of the FCP should have to be modified or should suffer. This leads to a paradox: the party that wants to create "socialism under the colors of France" has as its only criticism of Soviet foreign policy that it is too lenient toward French foreign policy.

Similarly, Professor Giuseppe Are of the University of Pisa pointed out in a lecture given at Rome in the fall of 1976 the role of Italy in international affairs:

It is impossible to find in the Italian Communist press an example of Soviet foreign policy initiative, action, or suggestion—vis-à-vis countries outside the Eastern bloc, to be more exact—that the Communist press considers contrary to détente, dangerous, aggressive, threatening, or worthy of criticism for any reason.

We might well have dispensed with this detailed analysis. No matter how embarrassing they find the internal problems of socialist countries, the Eurocommunist parties are obliged, sooner or later, to accept them anyway, as it has always been. It is just not possible to take credit for the good while shrugging off the bad. The Eurocommunist parties have to take the bath water as well as the baby, because communism in its very essence is internationalist. Over time the Communist movement has spawned differentiated national realities as with differing degrees of success it has been able to become naturalized. But its original worldwide dimension, even and especially where it has succeeded in creating an authentic national entity, constitutes the most important guarantee of its endurance. It is Berlinguer, as usual, who has found the most exact phrasing of this: "Without a vigilant internationalist spirit, the Italian working-class movement would lose its autonomy. It is not by chance that our opponents try to weaken our stance in that direction" (Rome, February 25, 1977).

6

Obstacles

If we now combine the analyses made of each of the three definitions and approaches to Eurocommunism, which are too often jumbled together, we can better find the terrain on which the entity that might take shape in the future under the name of Eurocommunism has chosen to rally its forces. One limit of this terrain is marked by liberal socialism "with a human face," another limit by a deliberately Europe-centered communism, and a third by "national communism." What are the chances that this as yet mostly undifferentiated embryo will be able to develop?

We can measure these chances by identifying the obstacles, threats, and assets that Eurocommunism will have to confront and to exploit to attain the status of a fully developed political reality that is operational and enduring.

There are at least three orders of obstacles.

The first is the Soviet Communist party's public and frequently expressed condemnation of Eurocommunism, made in the name of the Communist orthodoxy that the Soviet party defends by virtue of its self-proclaimed right of primogeniture and its power. Starting in August 1975, there has been a series of articles in this vein. K. Zarodov (*Pravda*, August 6, 1975), V. V. Zagladin (*Voprosi filosofii*, October 1975), Vitaliy Korionov (*Pravda*, January 24, 1976), Mikhail Suslov (*Pravda*, March 18, 1976), Zagladin again (*Pravda*, April 20, 1976), Boris Ponomarev (*World Marxist Review*, May 1976), and A. Victorov (*Pravda*, March 1, 1977) have tirelessly repeated that it is not possible to part from the Soviet way without leaving Leninism. Victorov's ideas sum up the major point:

> Several Communist parties in Europe and in other regions of the world have enunciated programs whose objectives are to bring about radical

reform of the economic structure of society, to create a democratic-alliance type of structure in which the government would be based on a union of leftist forces, on antimonopolist democracy, and on other elements. Such programs must play a role in the intermediate stages and transitional forms on the road to socialism, taking into account the specific conditions of each country.

There could be no better way of saying that the coming to power of a Union of the Left government would be just one step along the trail of taking power. This power would become "socialist" only on the day that the Communist party was in control. "Experience has shown," Victorov continues, "that it is impossible to attain socialism within a bourgeois state or a bourgeois democracy. History furnishes many examples, the most recent of which is Chile." As for parliamentary victory, that would give the workers only the appearance of power: "The real power in society rests with those who control economic power, the machinery of state, and the army. And this power is in the hands of the bourgeoisie." It is therefore necessary for the workers to "transform parliament from an instrument of bourgeois hegemony to an organ that expresses the interests of the workers." The workers are to use a "peaceful kind of violence" in the format of "expropriation of large property-holders, abolition or limitation of the political rights of the exploiting classes, and imposition of obligatory work for these classes." To direct this indispensable process of transition from capitalism to socialism, "the Marxist-Leninist parties play an important role in the formation of the mass political army of the revolution. These parties derive their power above all from their unity, their unshaking loyalty to the principles of Marxism-Leninism, and their international solidarity."

Is there anything new in all this? Of course not, and it is the very absence of any new elements that characterizes this type of writing. Is this nothing more than a repetition of dogma? To be sure, but does it suffice to respond that we are tired of dogma? What if adherence to dogma was solely responsible for past successes, and if ignorance of dogma had always led to failures? And finally what if there were no other serious theoretical reasons for the changes sought by the Eurocommunist leaders than their own loss of confidence and their opportunistic degeneration? In this regard they have had many predecessors, but the Communist movement has generally succeeded in sweeping them out of its way. In any case, the Soviet leaders are convinced of the truth of the preceding litany. They note with interest that Eurocommunist ideas issue from the highest levels of the Western party structures. These are the same levels that of necessity are in contact with the dominant and established political society of which they are a part, and they run the risk of being contaminated or even of being absorbed. In contrast, the ordinary rank-and-file workers who make up the mass support of the parties remain for the most part indifferent to Eurocommunism and maintain their respect and affection of the socialist world such as it is because it is their world.

The second obstacle is the rigid nature of the Communist image in Western Europe. There the public has formed a fixed image of communism during the sixty years that it has existed in all of Western Europe. It is irrelevant whether this image is positive or negative; what counts is that the public seems little likely to revise it. We saw the proof in the Paris Fifth Arrondissement election campaign in the fall of 1976 (where the Communist candidate was Jean Elleinstein); electoral democracy remains hostile to Eurocommunism and does not evince interest in distinguishing between liberal-minded neo-Communists or hard-line "paleolithic" Communists.

There is a serious problem here, for Eurocommunism may be more than the manifestation of a desire to win votes. The interpretation that it is only a tactical calculation designed to fool voters cancels out its more authentic motivation: to grope toward another model of socialism, not because the new model would be more likely to please the voters but because it would correspond better to the initial expectations of militant revolutionaries. Nevertheless, even if electoral ambitions were not its sole motivation, Eurocommunism must still seek the only proper validation obtainable in democratic society—electoral validation.

If communism does find itself in decline in the West, the first indicators would be the beginning of a breakdown of loyalty on the part of the traditional Communist electorate. Communist terminology employs the word "compression" [*tassement*] to describe a stagnation, if not an outright retreat, of electoral support. At present there is nothing to prove that Eurocommunism is capable of reversing that tendency. The results obtained by the Communist party in Spain, which of the three parties is the most thoroughly engaged in Eurocommunism-style revisions, were quite disappointing: less than 10 percent of the voters went Communist. The Italian Communist party has no greater assurance that its well-publicized Eurocommunism will ward off the decline projected by some sources. In France, as we shall explain in greater detail subsequently, Eurocommunism is only the complement of a Popular Front-type strategy whose theory as well as practice is considerably older than the emergence of the Eurocommunist phenomenon. However, it should be pointed out that the Popular Front-type strategy had been specifically developed for the Communist parties of Western Europe, especially those of Spain and France, before being extended to other sectors. This historical aspect of the strategy is often overlooked today.

To be sure, the results obtained by the FCP in the municipal elections of 1977 led analysts to conclude that thanks to Eurocommunism of the FCP, "the French were no longer afraid of Communism." This finding is premature. It simply can't be proven that the French no longer fear communism as such; what they are not frightened of is the possibility of government by the Union of the Left. The public seems to feel that the Socialist majority would be able to hold off any foreseeable attempts on the part of the Communists of revolutionary activity. Whether they were right or wrong does not really matter here.

The most that we can say about the Eurocommunism of Georges Marchais is that it has assured everyone that the secretary-general of the French Communist party, by aligning himself openly with the important Eurocommunist preoccupations, showed that he knew what was expected of him.

The third obstacle, finally, is the lack of a loophole. While the advanced state of collapse of the non-Communist Left in Italy gives the ICP a fairly large field for maneuvering, the situation is different for the Spanish and French Communist parties. Limited on their right by all sorts of democratic socialist movements (including "left-socialism" of neo-leftist or proto-Communist origin), and on their left by the proliferation of leftist groups (Marxist, neo-Marxist, anarchist, etc.), the French and Spanish parties have very little room for political maneuvering.

The Communists have to deal with the Socialist party on matters of internal policy and with the Gaullist movement on the nationalist issues, although de Gaulle's death has induced some moderation on the part of the nationalist flag-wavers in his ranks. Nevertheless, it cannot be said that there is room for maneuvering on the nationalist question and that the FCP might be able to take over this position. The Spanish Communist party has some major problems on this issue, where the field is crowded not just by Spanish nationalism but by the nationalisms of the different Spains.

In short, the alloy of verbal radicalism, practical reformism, and strategic nationalism, besides being likely to break down because of the inherent incompatibility of its components, is not capable of providing its own legitimacy. It cannot serve as a substitute for the legitimacy through which communism has acquired, in some European capitalist countries, its capacity for endurance: the identification of communism with the emancipation of the working class.

7

Threats

Let's move now from the obstacles to the threats, of which there are at least two.

The first is that the Soviets may decide not to put up with an autonomist trend that they have been obliged to tolerate for a certain time.

It was natural for them to temporize at first, because they had to take the measure of their opposition: the preparatory phase of the pan-European Communist conference gave them the opportunity. After the Italian Communist party delegation agreed in Moscow early in 1973 that the time was right for convocation of a pan-European Communist conference, and after the leaders of the East German, Hungarian, and Bulgarian parties stated in December 1973 that "the time had come" for another world meeting, to be preceded by a pan-European meeting, an endless ballet of secret bilateral consultations, multilateral consultative meetings, and preparatory gatherings (at least sixteen within twenty months) got under way. Although the grandiose initial plan was for the conference to convene nearly simultaneously with the celebration of the thirtieth anniversary of the victory over fascism, it was not until June 1976, a year after the Helsinki Security Conference between both Communist and non-Communist *states*, that the conference of Communist *parties* was finally convened, in East Berlin. This shows how much more delicate and problematical it was to bring together the heads of Europe's Communist parties, in or out of power, than it was to assemble the leaders of socialist and non-socialist Europe.

Briefly in the spring of 1975, the study group charged with drawing up the agenda and the proposed final text sought to name a subgroup made up of delegates from eight parties, the four "dissidents" (Yugoslavia, Romania, Italy, and Spain) and four "orthodox" parties (the Soviet Union, East Germany, France, and Denmark), in order to bypass some bottlenecks. The efforts came to naught. The problem was that the Soviets, in keeping with the tradition of the international Communist movement, wanted the final document to lay out a "general line" that all fraternal parties would have to follow. The dissidents, who would have been willing to dispense with any final document at all, were agreeable only to a document that treated the struggle for peace and détente, that reaffirmed clearly the principles of autonomy, equality, and noninterference in relations between parties, and that would have been non-ideological, free from compulsion or condemnation of any party, even that of China.

The Soviets seemed hesitant, even dumbfounded, at several points. One might conclude that they were even in disagreement among themselves about the conduct of negotiations, on the importance and the nature of concessions that were worth accepting. What is certain is that their representatives blew hot and cold: Ponomarev and Zagladin tended to blow hot, while Katuchev blew cold. They had to admit, finally, that the conference would take place without being a decisive show of orthodoxy; on the contrary, the conference was a demonstration that diversity had acquired, in the heart of the European Communist movement, a quasi-institutional status. This was quite a change from the last conference of this type, which took place in the spring of 1969. At that time the only indication of decline in Soviet control was that several parties refused to sign the mutual declaration, while others, including the Italian and Romanian parties, signed only a portion of the document, or signed with reservations.

But it remains to be seen whether the Soviets have for the moment given up on their plan of repelling dissidence step-by-step.

They first had to drive the evil out from the very center of the world Communist movement, where it had blown up after Stalin's death. In the Soviet Union a selective and arbitrary policy of repression, stopping short of mass assassination but using ostracism against the recalcitrants, has been successful up to now in holding internal opposition to an endurable level. The price, of course, has been higher than the originators of the policy expected. Contrary to their calculations, both the Jews, who had demanded the right to emigrate "to join their historic country," and the banished dissidents of all persuasions—Christians, liberals, nationalists, Trotskyites, and neo-Marxists—did not, once they had left the socialist world, turn their backs on those who were left behind to suffer. They did not sink into dereliction and silence, nor did they let themselves be seduced by the debauchery and corruption of the Western world. Further contrary to their calculations, the originators of this policy find that it no longer suffices to behead or dishonor the democratic movement: a new head always appears, and honor always regenerates. And especially contrary to their expectations, they have discovered that Western public opinion, instead of becoming saturated and bored by the complaints and whimperings of the victims, has been enlivened by the courage and the dignity of these new martyrs, who stand on the principles of 1789. This was true even to the point where the president of the United States, just installed in office, stated in an official letter to Sakharov that he was determined to reject the Kissinger-type *Realpolitik* on this matter: "You can rest assured that the people and the government of the United States will pursue their efforts to contribute to respect for the rights of man"—a gesture and statement that caused alarm throughout the Western diplomatic establishment concerned with détente.

But one should not conclude from all this that the Soviet situation might escape the control of established power: the democratic movement itself is under no illusion that it is fighting a colossus with feet of clay. It was not necessary to learn of the tenor of the warnings given by the Soviet Communist party to the Italian and French parties on the eve of the Madrid conference in March 1977 to be convinced that the Soviet government, if it did not banish its dissidents, was determined to treat them as hostages.

It was next necessary to drive out heterodoxy from the buffer zone of socialist states. This was a difficult task, even with periodic recourse to direct military intervention or brutal repression. The October Revolution had been Russian enough to give satisfaction to the national energy of Russian culture. The revolution also had the effect of deeply eroding Russian society so that, with its very vitality maimed, it was barely able to keep body and soul together under Soviet rule.

In the people's democracies, by contrast, the insult to nationhood and the persistence of autonomous social vitality condemn the socialist edifice to an eternally precarious existence. Even though industrial modernization was helped to wear down the indigenous culture, the apparatus of socialism still resembles a superstructure added as an afterthought. In the early years, the faith of a small band of devoted Communists and the fear of the large majority allowed the socialist apparatus to be tolerated. But the faith eroded, and fear has disappeared: as François Fejtö has emphasized, Solzhenitsyn has triggered off a fantastic "spiritual revolution" by showing how one can fight against fear. We find a cyclical return, almost every decade, of the confrontation between society and established power: the censorship that hides real knowledge of the events of recent history paradoxically contributes to the erasure from the public memory of recollections of past repressions, so that each young generation does not have to get out from under the weight of disillusion and bitterness born of past failures.

Consequently, as in Poland, wherever a powerful native workers' movement had earlier forged a working-class consciousness, the workers succeed—Danzig, Gdynia, Elblag, and Szczecin in December 1970, for example—in waging battles on such economic questions as sudden increases in food prices. These struggles mesh effortlessly with the protests of the intellectuals against the "state philosophy." This kind of philosophy, according to Cardinal Wyszynski, colored the amendment proposals for the Polish constitution with such expressions as "The Communist party is society's leading force in the elaboration of socialism," and with statements of "friendship" between Poland and the USSR.

And wherever the nationalist movement had in former days been able to free the nation from oppression, an intelligentsia would rise, draw tenaciousness from its utter hopelessness, and rediscover its earlier function of being the heroic spokesman for liberty in the struggle against oppression. But the vigor and especially the simultaneity of the confrontation taking shape once again between society and established power in the greater part of Central and Eastern Europe should not make us forget that the Soviet Union continues obstinately and successfully to follow its plan of reinforcing its control over the community of socialist states.

While China keeps its distance from this community, Romania and Yugoslavia have finally decided to join it, albeit on the periphery, as signified by Yugoslavia's participation in the June 1976 pan-European conference, its first such participation since 1957. Romania and Yugoslavia have no doubt won several concessions, notably to maintain close relations with each other; to maintain direct relations with the West (and with China, since the restoration of relations between China and Yugoslavia in 1968); and, finally, to maintain direct relations with the Third World.

But even if they view their participation as a means of getting around a possible front erected against them by the Soviets, these states run the risk of being obliged to participate in the activities of a community whose methods of integration have taken on increasingly cavalier diplomatic forms. According to Vasil Bil'ák, the reason Katuchev, who until recently had been in charge of relations between the Soviet Communist party and other parties in power, has just been named as the Soviet representative to COMECON was that "he is capable of finding the political means to effect a rapprochement between member states and especially to increase the integration of Romania and eventually of Yugoslavia."

The new treaty with East Germany, like the Czech treaty in 1973, contains two clauses of interest: the first legitimizes in advance the Soviet Union's right of intervention in order to preserve "Soviet conquests"; the second extends the "German treaty" to all frontiers of the Soviet bloc. According to the detailed analysis of the Communist community by Richard Szawlowski (*The System of the International Organizations of the Communist Countries* [Leyden, 1976]), since 1959, when Khrushchev spoke for the first time of a "single socialist system," its integration under Soviet control had been continually reinforced. In addition to the Warsaw Pact and COMECON, there are now about thirty interstate institutions that control transportation, energy supply, coordination and standardization of production, military equipment, and other aspects of cooperation.

The forms of integration in the military, economic, and ideological categories have become so forced—as shown by the "ideological" conference in Sofia, held in response to the Madrid Eurocommunist conference in March 1977—that one wonders whether Soviet leaders are planning eventually to give this community political dimensions. In any case, now that the "Brezhnev doctrine" has articulated the theory of "limited sovereignty," this is what the appearance of the new and surprising concept of *socialist internationalism* suggests.

The leaders of the Western Communist parties, who are out of power and therefore excluded from such a community, opposed the new notion. The possible political dimension of this community was brought up by Vladimir Kostov, a Bulgarian network journalist who requested political asylum in France. According to Kostov, in July 1973 the Central Committee plenum of the Bulgarian Communist party approved secret directives for the development of an integration plan that would allow Bulgaria, in the words of Todor Zhivkov, "to breathe at the same rhythm and use the same circulatory system as the Soviet Union." In Kostov's

_gration would lead to "the liquidation of independence and
_overeignty and the incorporation of Bulgaria in the USSR."
_t is left are the fringe areas of the Communist movement; more
_ifically, the Communist parties in Western Europe. Do the Soviets
_ave just one concern here: to keep these parties under their control, in
order to deter them from corruption in "unconsecrated soil," or at least
to keep them from contaminating the people's democracies? That is a
simplistic view, because if control is to be permanent and centrally
directed, it has meaning only if it does not interfere with regular
processes: except in extreme cases, there is no point in exercising control
over "political dead bodies." The Soviets therefore are less likely than
anyone to underestimate Eurocommunism's initial promises of adaptation, acclimatization, and renewal. They see that Eurocommunism might
serve to justify, as did the partial success of the EEC, a corresponding
increase in the cohesiveness of COMECON. Moreover, they observe that
Eurocommunism might favor the progressive development and growth
of technical, financial, and technological aid from Western Europe to the
Eastern bloc. The Italian example is instructive here: Fiat built a
production facility in Togliattigrad. Finally, the Soviets consider that
Eurocommunism is a much more authentic and native method than
Russian communism for achieving power in Western Europe.

But it would still be necessary for the process to remain compatible
with control. And it would be necessary to evaluate periodically the
potential conflict in the tension between policy and strategy to decide
whether or not intervention would be needed to redress the balance in
favor of control. What form might this intervention take? It would
certainly not be military intervention. In the near future, the death of
Tito and the subsequent shake-up of Yugoslavia in the context of
relations between socialist states is the only thing that could maintain
the desired contiguity with a Eurocommunist Italy. The defenders of
orthodoxy have the means, less expeditious and less massive, perhaps,
than direct intervention, but efficient nevertheless, to upset from the
outside anything they might find too distasteful.

We have already seen, in the aftermath of 1956 and 1968, how opposi-
tions or liberal majorities in the Communist parties of Austria, Norway,
and Sweden have been broken up and destroyed, sometimes at the price
of costly party splits. To be sure, these pro-Soviet ventures have not all
been successful. There was a failure in Japan in 1964 when the Soviet
Union overtly supported "antiparty" elements by helping them to

publish a newspaper, *The Voice of Japan,* which *Pravda* called "the paper of true patriots," and in Spain the effort also failed in an early phase when General Lister's pro-Soviet group was ousted in 1970. Nevertheless, the Soviet Union has expended much carefully orchestrated energy in these efforts. It was too bad that Greek communism broke into two parties: the orthodox KKE (exterior) group and the KKE (interior) faction, which resembles the fraction of the French PSU [Unified Socialist party] composed of former Communists, many of whom had worked in the Resistance. It was too bad that the Swedish party split in its turn in February 1977. In this case, the orthodox minority broke off, with the support of the Lapland miners and the workers of Malmö and Göteborg, and took as its title the Workers Communist party, abandoning the traditional name VPK [Left-Party Communists] to the Eurocommunist-dominated majority. The pro-Soviet Communist group in Surrey similarly created a "new Communist party" in July 1977 to distinguish itself from the "revisionism" of the Communist party of Great Britain, whose general secretary, Gordon McLennan, wants to return to the "British path to socialism" of the postwar period.

Once more we perceive that the Soviets are practical when it comes to unity or schism; they make their choice according to the situation and according to what is most important at the moment. The pace is moving so rapidly that the Western Eurocommunist parties do not even have the chance to get in step. The Spanish Communist party prefers to maintain warm relations with the Greek "interior" party; the Italian party tries to balance its policy by maintaining at least minimal relations with the Greek "exterior" party. As for the French Communist party, following its criterion of "noninterference in the domestic affairs of other parties," it recognizes only the official party in a given country. Therefore in Greece the FCP recognizes the pro-Soviet group, whereas in Sweden it has relations with the Eurocommunist party.

At the present point in its quarrel with the Eurocommunists, the Soviet Communist party appears to be willing to use only three means of applying pressure.

The first is indirect. The Soviets request the intervention of certain orthodox Communist parties who use the weight of their moral standing and exceptional prestige earned either from their disasters or from their triumphs. The Vietnamese and the Cuban parties are examples. This perhaps explains Marchais's concern for demonstrating his friendship

for Castro and his affinity for vacations in Cuba. The Chilean party is
another example. The Soviet Communist party got it to condemn dryly
the FCP's attitude in the Corvalán-Bukovsky case.

We have to admit that Marchais, by criticizing as "lamentable" the deal
between Brezhnev and Pinochet that brought about the mutual release
of Corvalán and Bukovsky, was curiously betraying tradition in such
matters. It has always been the rule that a Communist party secretary-
general would never be left in the hands of an enemy, no matter what
price the enemy demanded to obtain his release, even, and especially, if
this captive leader had failed to save his party from being caught on the
reefs of counterrevolution. A secretary-general, after all, represents
revolutionary legitimacy, which neither the voters nor the Communist
militants can represent, and he carries in his person the hopes of revival
for his party.

Moreover, once Corvalán was freed he went beyond merely refuting
Marchais's derogatory interpretation. This former inmate of Pinochet's
concentration camps delivered a vicious attack against the former
inmates of Soviet prison camps. In words right from the Cold War,
Corvalán said, "I understand why the Soviet Union has to defend
itself. . . ." He used the situation to treat the Eurocommunist strategy
lightly, saying in a bantering tone, "The Marchais line? I don't know
what that is." Corvalán also used the old saw about implied complicity
between Soviet opponents and fascism:

> Contrary to what one too often thinks in Western Europe, one doesn't
> show independence from Moscow by swelling the ranks of those who
> pick through Soviet affairs looking for errors and monstrosities. There
> are errors and monstrosities everywhere. I have better things to do than
> to scrutinize the affairs of a country that supports the struggle of my
> people. Do you want to hear all my thoughts? Well, I'm upset, because
> divisions between fraternal parties, attacks led against the Soviet Union
> by some Communists, destroy our united front and play the game of all
> the Pinochets.

Things had reached a pretty pass. The FCP did get Corvalán to
disavow the remarks attributed to him by the *Nouvel Observateur*, and in
return Corvalán agreed to a public reconciliation with Marchais.

The second kind of action available to the Soviet Communist party is
to make it known that its objections are shared by many people in the

upper ranks of the dissident parties and that it still maintains uncondi-
tional friendships among significant groups of party militants. The
"revered widows" come immediately to mind: the Soviet Embassy receives Gilberte Duclos with a great show. Jeannette Thorez-Vermeersch,
faithful to the priorities that she has maintained throughout her life,
published an article in *Le Monde* under her signature, and directed
against Elleinstein in particular, that presented the Soviet arguments.
One also thinks of militants who by the nature of their functions represent real worker opinion: in March 1977, the Supreme Soviet of the
USSR marked the fiftieth birthday of Georges Séguy, the secretary-
general of the CGT, by awarding him the Order of the October
Revolution.

The third category of possible actions is less pleasant. It is not out of
the question that, at a particular time, the Soviet Communist party would
have recourse to less symbolic and more sordid, but not necessarily less
effective, forms of pressure. Using ad hominem attacks against trouble-
some party leaders who are themselves prone to use such attacks is one
method. The Soviets have a large stock of biographic information about
non-Soviet Communist leaders that they can use, or misuse, to unleash
campaigns of public vilification. Georges Marchais's determination to
pursue his court case against people who have charged him with being a
voluntary worker in Germany in 1942 is not based just on French
internal-political imperatives. And if the secretary-general himself is not
the target, his staff and colleagues might be implicated: repeated
rumors have charged that Marchais's closest collaborators have certain
proclivities that the Communist party has always shunned.

Finally, it is certainly too late to exercise financial pressure on the
French and Italian Communist parties, whose income from their industrial and business holdings are as diversified as those of other con-
glomerates in the Western world, depending little on East—West trade.
Other parties, however, such as the Spanish Communist party, do not
have the luxury of a similar financial infrastructure and are more open
to threats. Will Eurocommunist solidarity be able to substitute for the old
form of solidarity in this domain as well?

Anyway, the Soviet Communist party does not intend simply to use
these carefully graduated methods at random; it plans to use them with
great discernment. Although it attacks Eurocommunism in general on a
doctrinal level, it is very careful not to confront the Eurocommunist
parties themselves on every terrain.

In this vein, it deals gently with the Italian Communist party. It is not entirely because of Berlinguer's urbanity that relations between Brezhnev and Berlinguer remain friendly. It is not only because of the warm welcome Corvalán received in Rome that he said, "Oh, I really like Berlinguer, I love that Italian party!"—even if the Italian party is no more satisfied by the terms of his release than the French party. The Soviet attitudes toward and actions involving the Italian Communist party reflect the fact that it is now something more than a party. The indirect role it plays in the survival of the Christian Democratic government and the direct role it occupies in the administration of regions and cities places the ICP in an intermediate position between opposition and power. To a certain degree it is already approaching the status of a party-state. Its sensitive situation justifies many concessions; and it would be foolish to barrage it with demands to toe the line when it is in the middle of a subtle acrobatic performance. As Corvalán, once again, says:

> I am enthusiastic about this notion of historic compromise. But what is Berlinguer doing? Exactly what we tried to do. We always sought contacts with the Christian Democrats, starting with Frei's period in office. I won't hesitate to say that we Chilean Communists were precursors.

In effect this is just a way of saying, "All we can do is hope that things work out better for you here than they did for us in Chile."

This indulgence toward the ICP hardly compares with the bitterness shown toward the French Communist party, according to the official report presented by Vasil Bil'ák to the Central Committee of the Czech Communist party in March 1977. First, the Soviets had no expectations at all of such eccentricity on the part of the French. Moscow was literally outraged when it observed that the French comrades, who had been known for their serious, solid, and sometimes even timorous qualities, were slaloming their way from right to left and back again through the international Communist movement.

But the Soviets are realistic: The FCP might also soon discard its status of opposition party, far removed from all centers of power, both governmental and nongovernmental. If the united Left wins in the coming elections, the FCP might become a governmental party. The July 10, 1977, issue of *Pravda*, moreover, expressed satisfaction at the recent successes of the French and Italian Communist parties. So in an uncertain period the Soviets have modified their attitude toward the

French fraternal party: without going so far as to extend warm or even cordial gestures, they have attained a kind of nonintervention, a "neither war nor peace" situation that will be displaced in one way or another when things become more clear.

It is all the easier for the Soviets to take a wait-and-see attitude toward the French party because they have a perfect target—the Spanish Communist party. Leninist strategy recommends breaking the chain by striking at the weakest link, and the Spanish Communist party fits that description exactly. Once past the period of reestablishment of democracy in Spain (the period during which the incomplete state of political institutions gives more weight temporarily to nonparliamentary mass action), the Spanish Communist party has shown itself for what it really is—a very small party. Both the Spanish and Portuguese parties have 150,000 members, although the Spanish population is three times that of Portugal, and is more urbanized and industrialized. As for electoral support, the Spanish party, which has not yet passed through a difficult revolutionary period, represents less than 10 percent of the voters, whereas the Portuguese party has the backing of more than 15 percent, even after its unsuccessful bid for power in 1975.

But, above all, the Spanish Communist party offers to the Soviets an opportunity to denounce "Eurocommunism in its pure form." Indeed, in its French and Italian form, Eurocommunism, as we will explain later, encompass or increase the credibility of anything: it exists by and for French and Italian parties: the Union of the Left and the historic compromise. Spanish Eurocommunism, by contrast, does not seek to encompass or increase the credibility of anything: it exists by and for itself. This is what Carrillo meant when he stated, "I'm guided by theoretical considerations." While Berlinguer and Marchais speak of Eurocommunism only in passing, and usually in response to questions from reporters, Santiago Carrillo went to the trouble while he was living clandestinely in Madrid, where he had returned shortly after Franco's death, of writing a book, *Eurocommunism and the State*, which was published in April 1977. In it he differs from his French colleague, who abruptly abandoned the dictatorship-of-the-proletariat concept out of motives of opportunism, failing to replace the notion in theory. Carrillo also abandons the concept, but only after weighing carefully what the record of the dictatorship of the proletariat has been where it has actually developed—in the USSR. According to Carrillo, the concept led to the formation of "a bureaucratic establishment that at every level has exaggerated and virtually uncontrolled political power. It makes decisions over the head of the working class and even of the party." Carrillo then develops a vigorous analysis of the "deviations" and "degeneration" he finds in the Soviet state and in its operations. In his book we find a Eurocommunism that is unlike that of either France or Italy: a kind of unrestrained leftist anti-Sovietism.

But Carrillo doesn't stop there. Unlike the French Communists, he considers it insufficient simply to stand pat on Communist attachment to democratic freedoms. He theorizes what a Western socialist democracy might look like by trying to distinguish, in a manner that is at times neither very clear nor very convincing, between the Eurocommunist concept of society and the traditional social-democratic views.

It is under these conditions that the Soviets—using to their profit the fact that the first democratic elections in Spain have shown the marginal character of a Communist party that, in spite of its appeal abroad, does not appear to respond to Spanish needs at the moment—decided to roll out the big guns of orthodoxy. An article in the Soviet weekly *Novoie Vremia* [New Times] on June 23, 1977, underscored the basic idea: if Eurocommunism serves to "designate the particularities of the strategies of certain Communist parties," there's nothing wrong with that, but there's nothing new, either:

> The Soviet Communist Party has always emphasized the importance of taking specific circumstances into account in determining the actions to be taken by Communists in the development of the strategy of revolutionary struggle. It is natural that Communist parties in the developed Western countries, as well as other Communist parties, pay careful attention to the national and historic conditions of the development of their countries.

But if Eurocommunism applies to "some nameless type of Communism," that just will not do: "Communism, real, scientific Communism, is unique."

Moscow's proposed distinction is astute. It is also well drawn: Moscow's theoretical and ideological condemnation is not of a *political action* by a *party*, whose autonomy Moscow does not challenge, but of a *conception* of Socialist power described by a *book* that purports to be doctrinal. The distinction, once drawn, immediately showed its effectiveness: although the Spanish party immediately closed ranks around its secretary-general, the French and Italian parties did not exactly run to the rescue, to say the least. Marchais did state, "We're not going to move an inch," but it was a question of the French party's position, not that of the Spanish party. Similarly, *Unità* pointed out "unclear and ambiguous" parts of the *Novoie Vremia* article. But it is not certain that the unclear and ambiguous elements were not on the Eurocommunist side. Moreover, this was the moment chosen by the Italian Communists to send an official delegation to Moscow. This was a high-level delegation headed by one of their old-time leaders, Giancarlo Pajetta, chairman of the International Policy Committee of the ICP. The top Soviet specialists in this area, Suslov, Ponomarev, and Zagladin, met with the delegation. Finally, both the French and Italian Communist parties are careful not to discuss the fundamental issues at hand: in 1968 what they criticized was Soviet military intervention in Czechoslovakia, not the intervention itself, just as in 1977 they express regret at the tone and "the manner in which the Soviet side has conducted the exchange," because "this manner does not encourage discussion and debate."

So the threat of Soviet intervention does weigh upon the Eurocommunist parties in one form or another. What makes this threat even more menacing is that it draws substance from a second threat whose shadow falls upon each of these parties—the threat of foundering in a crisis of identity and of coherency in the process of moving away from the source of Soviet orthodoxy.

The identity crisis lurks in the fear of an eventual fading away from a sense of belonging to a world, part of whose prestige stems from a special meaning it gives to its members and from a mechanism of identification it imparts to its entities: the working class, the revolution, peaceful and united humanity, perfect society, and the pursuit of justice and happiness. These characteristics serve to fulfill the individual in contemporary society so that he might recognize himself in the mirror of a collective universal adventure.

There are signs at present that indicate a growing concern for identity: when the FCP takes up for its own use such issues developed by other leftist forces as ecology, it is not fully supported by its traditional electorate, the workers, who do not want to see a bucolic utopia replace the old utopia of an industrial society in which the people would control the wealth.

From this we can see the danger in rushing too quickly into the sensitive question of sorting out what is really Communist and what comes from the Soviet experience. A SOFRES poll taken in June 1977 on the image of the Soviet Union in France shows how clearly the Communist voters stand apart from all other voters on this subject: whereas 20 percent of people expressing preference for the Communist party have *a lot* of sympathy for the Soviet Union (and 55 percent have *a little* sympathy), only 3 percent of Left-Socialist supporters, 2 percent of Radical party supporters, and 5 percent of RPR [Rally for the Republic, a right-wing Gaullist group] supporters favor the former position. Further, it was found that 17 percent of Communist supporters considered Soviet performance with regard to civil and individual liberties to be "on the whole successful" (44 percent had no opinion).

It is the same with coherency. Every time that we have seen a pillar of the temple fall—the issue of the dictatorship of the proletariat is a fitting example—we have waited in vain for the cataclysm. Nevertheless, ideology holds a key spot in the communist world, and the ideologists occupy a privileged place in communist society. Although they bear no responsibility for creating or updating theories to keep in step with the passage of time or with social changes, they do at least have the function of commenting on and illustrating ideology. But what is the proper position of ideology? It is not part of the core of the precisely defined ideas of the Leninist system. Its place rather is in the conviction that the system must remain closed off so that no new elements from the outside can penetrate it without having been duly selected, tested, and then "naturalized." The force of theory in Leninism comes not from having placed imagination in the driver's seat but from having put guards at the door.

Only elements that threaten to break into the closed circular flow of ideology can constitute a challenge, and this, by the way, is what the Althusserian Thomists, for whom the letter is also the spirit, want us to remember.

The different parties involved have varying degrees of tolerance for the loss of identity or coherency. The Italian Communist party has always functioned as a kind of double heresy—a Protestant-type heresy vis-à-vis the Catholics, and a Hegelian- and Gramscist-type heresy vis-à-vis Leninist orthodoxy. It can tolerate the loss better than the French Communist party, which has always functioned as a kind of double orthodoxy—it offers itself as a substitute model for French society, and it is orthodox within the Communist movement, where it was long regarded the "eldest daughter of the Marxist church." At heart,

French political culture, which is itself permeated by Cartesian clarity—is not *clarification* the key word in contemporary French politics?—and the taste for positivist distinctions, finds it both distasteful and incongruous that communism in France floats like the franc.

The threat of Soviet intervention in the form of a major excommunication that would deny identity or coherency might cause a general condition of malaise and then the crystallization of a more or less structured internal opposition within those Communist parties in the process of Eurocommunization. Is this what Corvalán wanted to get across in his *Nouvel Observateur* interview?—"All the messages that I have received from French Communists make it clear that not everyone inside the FCP shares the position taken by the secretary-general."

One should be careful, however, in interpreting the indices that tend to suggest that this process has, effectively, been implemented. First, the slightest nuance, sign of reservation, or dissonance is not a sure indicator of an unavoidable conflict: even during the period of monolithic Stalinism there were discussions—within clearly established limits, of course—and struggles for power, even though it was clear that this power could be exercised only in an orthodox manner. Wisdom would have it, then, that we take note of and classify the indices of eventual hostility, but that we try not to draw any magisterial conclusions from them right now. It is important not to anticipate and to prejudge—from the plausible to the possible, from the possible to the probable, from the probable to the real. Berlinguer's situation in Italy bears this out. By arguing that he has all kinds of pressure on him and on his strategy from the left wing of his party and generally from its working class base, he can obtain more important concessions from the Christian Democrats.

Is this how we should also understand Marchais's joking observation concerning the problems caused when the Socialists asked for what, in his opinion, was more than their fair share of candidacies for the March 1977 municipal government elections?—"Comrades and friends are going to say, 'We told you so.' "

We cannot expect to see a well-structured opposition developing in the near future, because an opposition could only be fragmented and divided within itself and against itself. In the past sixty years, each crisis within the Communist party has given rise to a left opposition and a right opposition, and to schisms between those who consider the new development too timid and those who find it too bold, not to mention those who consider it the wrong development altogether. Consequently, the established leaders were always able to carry the day by keeping in the center of the chessboard, equidistant not from the opposition but from the opposition*s*. Moreover, this is perhaps what is radically new about developments in the USSR and the people's democracies. Sakharov, for example, deliberately abandoned the "revisionist" strategy of support within the party of a "liberal" wing against a "Stalinist" wing, because he had a profound insight—that the opposition should produce its platform of defense of human rights, since that platform is neither to the left nor to the right of the orthodox position, but is outside the orthodox dimension entirely.

Finally, so that we're not tempted to overestimate prematurely the strength of eventual internal opposition to the Eurocommunist leanings of the leadership, we should recall what the leadership's assets are in the struggle. First, "democratic centralism" is still in force, and the manner in which it governs Communist party operations gives the leadership a great advantage over the opposition, whether conservative, neo-Stalinist, or ultrarevisionist. As is well known, the most operational mechanism in this area is acceleration of the turnover rate of the militant base. Under normal conditions, 10 to 13 percent of members fail to renew their memberships from year to year for various reasons, making it necessary to obtain new members at the rate of 10 to 20 percent of the total membership to keep the party at regular strength or to increase its size. At this rate, it is not surprising that two-thirds or perhaps even three-quarters of the members of the Communist party at any given time are of relatively recent vintage. This proportion becomes even larger during an expansion phase, to the point where nearly all the party members join or become integrated into party activity within the period of change. In these conditions, doubts, uneasiness, and questioning are the prerogative of only a third, a quarter, or an even smaller portion of the party militants, who no matter what their age or length of membership can associate with the stable nucleus dominated by the party apparatus. These militants are the lower and middle-echelon bureaucrats who, as in any institution, tend to oppose innovation.

But wouldn't those most likely to be doubtful or uneasy about the new developments be reassured by the fact that the most ardent "Eurocommunists" today, those who set the tone and beat the measure, are not scatterbrained neophytes but established leaders who have grown old in harness? In the French Communist party, Georges Marchais, Jean

Kanapa, Paul Laurent, Gaston Plissonier, Georges Séguy, and Henri Krasucki, the entire decision-making group, all belong to the generation of the end of the forties and the beginning of the fifties, the generation that grew up under Stalinism. Similarly, during the Popular Front it was not the "new men" who took charge of speaking for democracy and the French nation after having for so long talked of the dictatorship of the Soviets and of Soviet patriotism; it was the men of the "first generation," those who had created the narrow Bolshevik sect in the period 1925−35, like Thorez, Frachon, and Duclos. It is not without interest to note that neither the Popular Front generation—the members who joined the party at the time of heady victory in 1936—nor the Resistance generation—the members who joined the party for reasons of nationalism and antifascism during the grim years—has furnished many permanent cadres to the party. The only two batches of long-term leaders came out of the two long crossings in the desert (1925−35; 1947−60), those who endured segregation and the ghetto out of loyalty to the Soviet Union and to the international Communist movement.

In this perspective we can understand now that the precocity of the Italian Communist party in formulating several of the initial Euro-communist concepts was responsible for the precocity of its many-sided malaise. During the winter of 1976−77 the leadership of the ICP was deluged with letters written by party members to state their confusion over the policy of supporting the Andreotti government. While some of these letters were fictitious, written either by non-Communists or by pro-Soviet Communists more or less under orders from the socialist states in an attempt to modify the decisions of the ICP, at least half of the letters were authenticated by verification of signatures, and several were published, including one from the Communist mayor of Vercelli.

This malaise and dissension are the expression of doubts and uncertainty not only about the correctness of the path chosen but also about its chances of success and the type of success that might result from it. The discord is serious enough that Berlinguer himself has slackened his pace for a respite before continuing. This, at least, is the impression given by his most recent speeches, which are full of the traditional expressions that he had allowed to fall into disuse. Moscow has found his recent speeches so agreeable that Vadim Zagladin quoted Berlinguer favorably three times in a single editorial on proletarian internationalism. Moreover, Berlinguer received with great ceremony Alvaro Cunhal and Luis Corvalán, the secretaries-general of the two parties that gave immediate approval to the Soviet intervention in Czechoslovakia in 1968, started unsuccessful "revolutionary processes" in their own countries in the seventies, and finally showed their indifference to the policy of repression in the Soviet Union and the people's democracies.

8

Three Scenarios

The very real obstacles and threats to Eurocommunism should not cause us to ignore the assets at the disposition of the Eurocommunist parties. It is only when we have calculated their role in the equation of Eurocommunism that we can speculate with some degree of accuracy about where Eurocommunism is likely to go from here.

The first asset is that Eurocommunism can be presented as a new and more sophisticated version of what used to be called *Finlandization*. To accept being Finlandized instead of being reduced to the condition of a people's democracy, or to accept being Eurocommunized instead of being Communized, may well sound attractive. But it would be necessary for the Communist danger to be immediate. Are we to that point? Let's look at the Italian case.

There is a host of reasons causing us to conclude that there would be no inevitable Communist takeover after the tentative and then formal stage of the historical compromise; nor that there would even be inevitable ministerial participation by Communists in a national union government: the elasticity of Italian political culture, for instance, as well as the non-centrality of the Italian state, and the capacity for hedging and shifting shared by all components of the political leadership and the electorate. Other factors weighing against the Communist encroachment include the advanced diffusion, dissemination, and interlocking of a multitude of different powers—the church, *confindustria*, the army, and the *bersaglieri*—and the abiding interest of American public opinion in Italian affairs, due largely to the Italian-American community. Above all, the extreme severity of the Italian economic crisis poses the question as to what miracle remedies the Communists can draw out of a hat. What might they do that the Christian Democrats have not already tried? And what means might they use to reestablish order—other than the means that they have made too much use of in the past?

The second asset is the threat of retaliation that the Western Communist parties can use against their Soviet counterparts by turning loose their own "plague" against the people's democracies. We should note, however, that they have not even been able to pass Eurocommunism on to all the Communist parties in their own region, most of whom remain obedient to Moscow. Eurocommunist support for dissidents in Poland or Czechoslovakia is no doubt a major indicator of the intensity of the struggle between convinced orthodox members and others leaning toward heresy. The Italian Communist party stood out early in the picture by its audacity in supporting the Romanian and Yugoslav protests against Soviet encroachments and its refusal to ratify the fable of Czech "normalization."

The FCP, by contrast, has long made clear—by reason of both its reservations on these subjects and its determination to maintain the hypocritical principle of nonintervention in the internal affairs of other parties—that it doesn't intend to play that particular card. During the spring and summer of 1976 it exercised considerable discretion in its treatment of Polish events. Things changed during the autumn and winter of 1976−77: its principal organ gave abundant coverage to the many different forms of dissidence in the people's democracies. However, especially since the question of human rights has become a major international issue, taken up in depth by the American government, there has been a falling off of Eurocommunist initiatives, and the Madrid conference in March 1977 pinpointed where the French and Italian parties have halted: they refuse to say *jointly* what they are willing to say *separately*.

Having reviewed the obstacles and threats to, and the assets of, Eurocommunism, what conclusions can we draw from this analysis? I think there are three possible scenarios.

According to the first scenario, after an uncertain period of trial and error, Eurocommunist control will be halted, to be followed by a generalized return to a more traditional orthodoxy. This would not, of course, rule out various degrees of internal rearrangement, modification, and enrichment in the form of changes in language (although it is not likely that the "dictatorship of the proletariat" will make a comeback), style, and emphasis on subjects that relate to the evolution of Western society; nor would it rule out the existence of residual localized pockets of heresy.

This is what happened to a number of Communist offshoots that appeared during and after the 1950s. Although the Chinese variety of communism has endured, this is undoubtedly less because of its internal consistency and particular resistance than because of the relative weight of China and the Soviet Union and the difference between the Chinese and Soviet rates of transformation. The principal point of dispute after Mao's death between the "Gang of Four" and the majority was not what was debated after Stalin's death in the Soviet Union (liberalization), but was instead the subject disputed after the death of Lenin (permanent revolution versus industrialization). And the outcome, inevitably, was the same. As for the Castroite variety of communism, it is on the verge of losing the qualities that made it autonomous. Except for its specialization on problems of the Third World, Castroism has, through its cynicism, become worthy of its Leninist model: Castro's dubbing of Qaddafi as a Socialist in March 1977—which was either farcical or painful, depending upon one's respect for the idea of socialism—shows how far Cuba has been integrated as an instrumentality of the Soviet game.

Finally, though the Yugoslav experience poses some questions about what its unique system of worker self-management consists of, the Titoist and Romanian varieties of communism are in precarious straits and wait the day of reckoning when their respective leaders are gone. (There is nothing whatsoever to query about the Romanian internal experience: today's princely family has clearly taken up the methods, style, and manners of the former ruling families of the principalities.)

After having aspired to shape a specific program designed to assure its autonomy as a possible prelude to independence, Eurocommunism might well return to a role more in keeping with tradition, in which it would simply designate the Western European portion of the world Communist movement. This realignment would be quite acceptable to Moscow, because the very heart of the Leninist system—the creation and functioning of avant-garde parties, of *Bolshevik* parties—would be maintained.

The French situation lends itself quite readily to this development. The Popular Front strategy, especially if it reaches a serious level with the coming to power of a Union of the Left government, would amply justify and excuse any distortions made in proletarian internationalism.

The French version of Eurocommunism, rightfully basing itself on the
Thorez precedents of 1937 and 1946—which as everyone knows did not
launch an independent Eurocommunist policy—would be content with
having been a vigorous and bold adaptation to the circumstances and
demands of a unique promising situation. This adaptation would be
similar to previous intrepid adaptations between 1934 and 1936, when
the FCP moved from revolutionary antipatriotism to neo-Jacobin patriotism and from the dictatorship of "Soviets everywhere" to antifascist
democracy.

These earlier adaptations had the approval, although at first reticent
and uneasy, of the Communist International, where the leadership engaged in lively discussions as to the opportuneness of such changes.
Manuilsky, who at the time was in charge of European affairs for the
Comintern and who supported the innovations of the French Communists, had the habit of muttering, "I'm risking my neck, I'm risking
my neck." He was able to save it, however, and somehow the Jacobin
patriotism of 1936 did not prove inconvenient three years later when in
1939 the German-Soviet Pact obliged the Comintern to state that the
war, contrary to what had been hoped for, would not be one of the
democracies against fascism but of imperialist powers fighting each
other; Communists, therefore, were to fall back to the "revolutionary
defeatism" policies of Lenin in the First World War.

If the overall return to orthodoxy does not materialize, then the
second scenario comes into play, requiring a new and strong effort so
that the process can continue to the point of rupture; this third schism
would make the Rome-Paris-Madrid triangle the fourth center (along
with Moscow, Peking, and Belgrade) of a Communist world that would
decidedly be in shreds. But such an escalation could take place only in the
very heart of Leninist doctrine: the Communist party's self-conception.
As long as the party sphere remains intact, there could well be internal
conflicts with Moscow, the germination of social-democratic processes—
as in Italy, where there has been considerable growth inside the party
apparatus of the state bureaucracy (elected officials from all functions
and levels; local and regional civil servants) at the expense of the traditional party or syndicalist bureaucracy, and the application of reformist policies. None of this is irreversible.

Nevertheless, at the first public meeting of the Central Committee of
his party, held in Rome in June 1976, Carrillo criticized the rigidity of

the cell—the basic unit of the party—and proposed to substitute for it new groups called *agrupaciones comunistas*. The Italians, similarly, have practically replaced the cell—especially the *work-site* cell—with the *territorial section* as the unit in which policy would be developed and implemented. And in 1970 the Japanese also modified their terminology, calling the cells *branches* and the candidate members *associate* members. All these changes are reminiscent of the semantic changes in France in 1936 when, in order to "naturalize" the French party and to anchor it more firmly to the tradition of the Great Revolution (of 1789, of course), the leaders substituted for the term *rayon*—borrowed directly from the Soviet Union—the term *section* to designate the intermediate entity between the cell, at the elementary level, and the federation, at the departmental level. So far no one has gone past the talking stage, and when Berlinguer addressed a typical Communist audience—the Milan metalworkers in February 1977—he fell naturally into the traditional language and topics of democratic centralism.

The French Communist party also intends to preserve this centralism, as shown by Paul Laurent's affected definition of the term. Laurent, a high party official in charge of organization, used a seemingly innocuous formula:

> Democratic centralism is defined by a double practice. The first is a discussion, a broad and democratic confrontation of opinion between all party members, in which all members participate in policy making. Second, once the discussion has ended and the decision has been made, it must be applied by all (*La Nouvelle Critique*, April 1977).

If democratic centralism were nothing more than a procedure for decision making that assured a just balance between deliberation and decision, then there would be nothing to worry about. In fact, however, it is something quite different: the sum total of the internal mechanisms that work for the sole benefit of the central leadership to gather information necessary for decision making, and the total mobilization of the militants for the elaboration of theory and practice and for the selection and training of persons working in the permanent and nonpermanent institutions of the party.

All the same, what is most lacking in this second scenario to make it plausible is the will to break off relations—on the Soviet side as well as the Western side. We must take into account that the Soviets refuse even to consider the idea of rupture. Once the idea was accepted, it could make of the Communist movement nothing more than a loose association composed of voluntary members who could withdraw at any time. This is why the Soviets still hope someday to obtain the solemn condemnation of China. They do not want China's withdrawal from the international Communist movement to be interpreted as the legitimate revision of a contract at its expiration; China must be punished for being dissident. The ambition for unanimity and the habit of unanimity remain central to Communist ecumenical sensitivity: it is through this means that the international movement functions as a country.

As for the leaders of the Western Communist parties, Marchais and especially Berlinguer never miss an opportunity to show that they are not looking for trouble. They would like to be relieved of the disgrace of supporting the burden of the Soviets' bad reputation, but eschewing support from the power of the socialist camp would be both vain and risky.

The most plausible theory is really the third one, in which things continue to follow their course. This would mean that there will be a long period, not of permanent revolution, but of permanent negotiations between the Soviet Communist party and the Western European parties.

In any case, Europe is not at present an immediate Soviet target. The kind of truce that the Soviets had declared after the death of Mao, in the vain hope that the new team would reverse the course of Chinese strategy, was dashed in February 1977. With the publication and approbation in *New China* of the statement by the commander in chief of American naval forces in the Pacific that American military presence is necessary "to counterbalance the Soviet military power in the region," Soviet and Chinese polemics became even more bitter than before Mao's death. And as long as Sino-Soviet relations stay on this level, the central focus of Soviet strategy remains the Indian Ocean and its two extensions, the Mideast and Africa.

The visit of President Nikolai V. Podgorny to Tanzania, Zambia, and Mozambique in the spring of 1977, after Castro's visit to Algeria, Libya, and Angola; the hurried recognition of Lieutenant-Colonel Mengistu in Ethiopia; and the alleged visit of a Cuban military mission in Uganda show that the Soviets do not consider Africa to be wasted time.

With the help of Cuba, Africa—the eastern sector, in particular—may well be the most likely source for new Soviet gains, although things are always somewhat doubtful because of the difficulty of winning over an

Africa in which the national state structures are still so largely super-imposed. In addition, by maintaining close relations with Uganda and Libya, by increasing their influence in Tanzania and Mozambique, and by focusing now on Kenya, the Soviets are weighing their investments closely, limiting themselves to strategic and military rather than political and economic objectives.

In these conditions, the Soviets have extended a certain degree of cautiously guarded laissez-faire to the Western Communist parties. It is basically a tactical compromise. The Soviets will not listen to Western parties' support of the Eastern dissidents, and the Westerners will not listen to Soviet criticism of Eurocommunism.

From our review of these scenarios it appears considerably premature at this point in the gestation of Eurocommunism to step forward and declare: "The child has been born and he will live." On the other hand, is it already time to declare, as *Le Monde* did on May 2, 1977, after having announced the birth of a healthy baby, that it was stillborn, taking note of "the liquidation in silence of a 'Eurocommunism' that never had much existence"? Executioner, please wait a moment.

9

What Would Happen If . . . ?

What would happen if . . . ? "The specter of Eurocommunism is haunting Western Europe."

The question is both inevitable and pertinent: this is the moment of truth.

But we still have to know what we're talking about. The chances of an electoral victory that will pull the Communists out of the opposition where they have been confined for exactly thirty years? The chances that the Common Program of the Left will be applied or that policies acceptable to the Left would be applied if a leftist, popular union, or national union government that contained Communist ministers would take over? The chances to throw into gear the process that would lead either directly or indirectly from a government in which the Communists play only a minority role to a government and power structure in which the Communist hegemony would be beyond dispute?

For one thing, it is starkly evident once we elucidate the different ways of pondering the pulsating question posed in the title of this chapter that the Eurocommunist dimension of the parties involved enters into play only at a secondary level.

I.

The first thing we need to make a satisfactory prognosis of the short-term possibilities of electoral victory is information about the relative strength of the different forces. The relationship between the two forces itself is the product of two major elements: first, the arithmetic sum of the portions that each party brings to the leftist coalition; second, the supplementary support rendered by the dynamics ensuing from the modalities and practice of the alliance. In fact it requires but a small internal shift in a Communist party undergoing Eurocommunization for there to be substantial modification in its final contribution to the alliance. What the alliance can gain in the dynamics generated by the Socialist-Communist rapprochement, which gives it a greater degree of homogeneity and credibility, the alliance can lose on the level of uniquely Communist support.

The Spanish Communist party has no chance at all, for two reasons. First, while its obstinacy has permitted it to survive Franco, the late dictator was able to reduce lastingly its popular support to the meager level attained before the beginning of the tragic Second Republic forty years ago. Second, Franco made sure that no one would forget either the disputes between Socialists and Communists or the enormous risks a revolutionary outcome from a leftist alliance involved. Whether Eurocommunist or not, the Spanish Communist party can do nothing (except to throw itself futilely into a revolutionary gesture that would be costly both for it as a party and for its members) to undo the fact that, although it managed to survive the Franco period, it remains stuck in a Spain that simply will not furnish support for an expansion of communism. Everything considered, in spite of the many different experiences of the European countries, there is a strong resemblance among the European political structures that succeeded dictatorships of the Right over the past half-century: Germany (divided, it is true, after having to give up its pound of flesh to the neighboring Communist Moloch) and Italy, after the apocalypse of Hitlerian nazism and the fascism of Mussolini, as well as Greece, Portugal, and Spain after the colonels, Salazar, and Franco, have reached a format of liberal democracy injected with a substantial dose of reformist socialism.

The chances of the FCP and the ICP winning a victory at the polls that would open the door to ministerial participation in the government are, to be sure, comparatively much greater. But as we said earlier, the possibilities for the ICP have not grown even though its Eurocommunization has become much more outspoken since 1975. There are a number of reasons for this. First, the party's working-class base has become somewhat uneasy about the party's determination to meet its expectations, which will suffer neither further delay nor evasion. Next, the political space to the left of the party has been occupied by a new form of political dissidence remaining outside of political as well as economic and social life because it represents those who cannot be integrated into the socioeconomic machine. Finally, the ICP has lowered its own expectations. After originally proposing a historic compromise, it later suggested a national-union or public-safety type of government; now it just wants the chance to participate in the government. However, it has lost its capacity to convince people that Communist ministerial participation would bring anything more to the government in the form of energy and vitality than it could get from simple nonparticipatory Communist support. The Italian Communist party has involuntarily conveyed the impression that it is no more capable, once it is willing to respect the methods of liberal democracy, than the other Italian political forces of imposing "law and order" and controlling the particular social and economic strata that are of its own leanings, if not its own followers.

No matter how brilliantly imaginative it often is, and no matter how likely it is to propose shortcuts and unexplored ways of proceeding, the strategy of the ICP remains all the more enigmatic because it has to deal with a situation for which the term *crisis* is an understatement. We might well wonder whether the Communist danger in Italy is not cooling for the simple reason that the real question is not whether the Italian state will go Communist but whether there will still be an Italian state. Another question worth pondering is whether the ICP's strategy has used up all its surprises before the party was able to reach its objectives.

Indeed, the Italian Communist party has succeeded in dismantling the Italian state in order to gain control over it piece by piece, but it is no longer able to put the pieces back together in order to benefit from the situation. The Italian Communist party is *in power*—except that there *is* no power anymore; what power does exist is in bits and pieces. The situation may not necessarily be unpleasant for the Italian population, but it certainly destroys Italy's role in international affairs. All that is left now for the major antagonistic powers of East and West is to use their "private" networks to take care of their own interests within Italy. Mussolini's sardonic phrase leaps unavoidably to mind: "How to govern Italians? It's not difficult. It's also useless." The drawbridge between civil society and the mysterious prince that is the Italian state is often raised. Conquering the surrounding society is only a diversion; it is still impossible to get across the moat that protects the prince, and no one knows for sure whether he really exists or is still alive.

As for the chances of the French Communist party, we have noted that its electoral decline, which was far from catastrophic, resembles rather a stagnant condition highlighted by pockets here and there of more marked erosion. Three principal factors have accentuated this stagnation: the exclusion from political society of the immigrant-worker portion of the proletariat and the subproletariat, who cannot vote; the decrease in population of those sectors of the working class involved in the old industries that have long had a fixed identification with the Communist party; and the technological diversification, intensification of geographic mobility, and growing complexity of socioeconomic hierarchies and situations, which have produced all sorts of subgroups and subcultures for which the FCP is not the sole political expression or means of identification.

The eighteen legislative by-elections held since 1974 illustrate this trend. As Georges Lavau has stressed, "The FCP did not win any of them; it gained votes in only five; and it came in first among the leftist candidates in only four."

Not even adoption of the Eurocommunist label could by itself compensate for this decline. It would have the contrary effect, because a diminished specificity of the Communist image would result. Once the sickle is afraid of its own cutting edge, and once it desires to rival the softness of the rose, why not simply avoid the long detour and settle for the rose? Once the sickle considers itself a rose, why wouldn't the rose say that it is by far the better model?

The example of the Japanese Communist party is quite suggestive from this point of view. From 1960 on the JCP launched an impressive campaign of Eurocommunization—before the term even existed—characterized by a double affiliation with democracy and independence. This process enabled the JCP to shed its reputation as a sectarian agitator. And while it was increasing its membership from 35,000 in 1958 to 350,000 in 1975, it received 10.5 percent of the votes and 38 seats in the 1972 legislative elections, compared with 4.8 percent of the vote and 5 seats in 1967. But now it seems frozen at the 1972 level, and it was bitterly disappointed by the results of the autumn 1976 elections, when it received 10.4 percent of the vote and 17 seats. The results of the July 1977 senatorial elections only confirmed and accentuated the disappointment; in elections for half the members of the upper house the number of Communist seats fell from 20 to 15.

The problem is that the Eurocommunization of the Japanese Communist party has developed without the concurrent development of some kind of alliance with the Socialists, who with only 50,000 members received 20.7 percent of the votes and 123 seats in the 1976 elections. Miyamoto Kenji cannot be faulted for not trying to develop a "United Front for Renovation"; however, none of the susceptible political forces— the Japanese Socialist party, the Komeito, or the Democratic Socialist party—has responded favorably to his proposal for a common governmental program.

For that matter, the FCP has not tried singlehandedly to boost its own electoral results. While in other circumstances it is very careful not to let itself be drowned in a sea of other parties and organizations, it was anxious to insinuate itself into common candidacies during the municipal election campaign in March 1977 so that it could simultaneously attain its three goals: first, to make it impossible to tell what its particular share of the common results were; second, to receive advantages from the leftist surge stemming from the dynamics of the union; and third, to get into the governments of as many as possible of those municipalities that previously had been governed by a Socialist-centrist coalition.

The third objective is itself not negligible. On one hand, the concomitant participation of Socialists in municipalities governed exclusively by Communists is rather small; and the Communist governance apparatus in municipalities under their control gives the Socialists little more than a symbolic role to play. On the other hand, above all, the concessions on both sides were not equal: there were 263 Communist candidates on Union of the Left lists in 26 cities of more than 30,000 residents that had formerly been administered by Socialist-centrist coalitions, whereas there were only 78 Socialist candidates on the Union lists in 10 cities of comparable size that were exclusively administered by Communists.

The major objective, however, is the second one. Indeed, the absolute-majority voting system automatically has more favorable results when the Socialist-Communist electoral alliance is in force, especially when the Socialist party has an ally on its right, even if the ally is unstable and temporary. In 1936, 1956, 1967, 1973, and 1977 both the Socialist and the Communist parties enjoyed electoral success, whereas in 1951, 1958, 1962, and 1968 both suffered losses.

But in order for the dynamics of the Union to come into play the Socialist party—and the Socialist candidates on the right and center of their party—must exercise the preeminent role. It took exactly forty years, nearly a half-century, for the constellation of the mid-1930s Popular Front to re-form, creating not just a Communist-Socialist relationship but a relationship in which the Socialists and right-wing Socialists have at least the appearance of control.

The example of Paris illustrates by contradiction the importance of this arrangement. The municipal elections were successful everywhere for the Left in 1977, but less so in Paris than in the provinces. In Paris as far back as the beginning of the century, and even during the period of Guesde and Jaurès, the Socialist party was a party of the provinces. It was weakly rooted in the capital, and it was extremist. Today the Communist voters in Paris are stronger than the Socialists, and the Socialists tend to be of the left-wing variety, the same faction that dominates the Seine Socialist Federation (which was already to the left, influenced by Marceau Pivert during the Popular Front when Osmin was its secretary).

There is no doubt that the Union of the Left, as it is conceived at present, will produce a greater increase both in votes and legislative seats for the Socialists than for the Communists. This drawback is inevitable. Things got so touchy in 1974 when it seemed that the Socialists were going to have considerable advantages over their partner in the alliance that the Communist party gave its angry supporters, who were exasperated by the problems of elaborating the Union, a year off, as it were, until the fall of 1975, to vent their hostility and say whatever they wanted to about the Socialists.

Nevertheless, the FCP expects to receive significant compensation for the Socialist advantages in votes and representation at the municipal and national levels, because the common electoral victory would allow it to increase in its favor the relative strength of organized militant forces. The FCP has stepped up its campaigns and membership drives since 1975 because in France periods of intense electoral campaigns heighten the people's interest in and appetite for militant activity; and when the outcome appears favorable it is all the easier to harvest a rich crop of new young members. In 1976 the FCP persuaded more than 100,000 people—the equivalent of a large city in France—to pick up a Communist card. In general terms two-thirds of these new members are under thirty; a third are women; and half are workers. Better yet, the figure of 100,000 new members was met in the first six months of 1977.

To be sure, in order to understand this significant increase in new memberships we must not overlook the fact that since the early 1960s the curve of FCP membership has risen slightly as compared with the continuous and substantial decline of the 1950s. Furthermore, we must not overlook the demographic factors that favor increased membership. The age cohorts between eighteen and thirty—which provide the greatest recruiting opportunity because political militancy is more often a choice at the beginning than at the end of one's adult life—are particularly strong in number, corresponding to the "baby boom" of the immediate postwar years. Another important political factor, one that is likely to remain permanent, is that women, after gaining the right to vote in 1945, started to engage in militant activity in the 1960s, late, perhaps, but with enthusiasm, so that the age cohorts in question are not only large in number but offer both sexes for political recruitment.

Finally, there are some important circumstantial political factors to consider. The FCP involved itself in every conceivable political struggle and issue, with no regard for the possibly unproductive nature or paltriness of the question. It thus won out over the leftist extremists, bringing most of them back into its ranks—a development that could have been foreseen as the 1970s began, given the volatile nature of extremist preoccupations and their indifference to discontinuity and incoherence. The party has further expanded its audience by carefully calculating just how much of the new it should add, to heighten the flavor, to the unchanging base structure. The Italian Communist party, by contrast, during the winter of 1977 suffered a severe loss of membership on the order of about 20 percent compared with the same period in the preceding year.

No one doubts, of course, that a substantial number of the new Communist members will not long remain in the party, having made their decision lightly, perhaps, or finding that they are not suited to their new political situation. But among the new recruits the number who will adapt to the continuous and extensive initiation period during which a young neophyte becomes a confirmed militant is sufficient to assure, as of now, that the party's base will be renewed and reinforced for the near future.

The mechanism the FCP has counted on to reverse the course of its electoral decline is thus *mutatis mutandis* (the strength of the Radical party having substantially declined from 1936 to 1976, even though middle-class strength has increased considerably), the same mechanism that worked in the mid-1930s. After the poor showing at the polls in the 1932 legislative elections, the party hoped to reverse the trend by forming an alliance in 1936 that would break away from the former "class against class" tactic and replace it with not so much a "united front" as a "single front" with the Socialists. The Popular Front of 1936 was the result.

II.

So what the FCP has in mind is a remake of the Popular Front, but the elaboration of the new system has required considerable expenditure of time and effort. The FCP has needed about fifteen years to put in place and tie together the different elements of a Popular Front or Union of the Left strategy in what looked like the best way on the basis of what the party had learned in the 1930s and 1940s.

Why was so much time needed? First, for a fundamental reason mentioned earlier: nothing could really be done as long as the Soviet Union and the international Communist movement viewed the Gaullist system as a useful contradiction in the heart of the capitalist world. Consequently, the French Communists found themselves obliged to play the role of an opposition force without having hopes of being part of a political alternative. As it has been progressively freed from this restriction on its action, the FCP, making as if to exaggerate the degeneration of Gaullism, has been able to advance its own interests.

And there was another reason why so much time was needed. Elementary political logic requires that there have to be Socialists in order to have a strategy of alliance between Socialists and Communists. The Communist party has always been actively concerned with the Socialist party—it tries to tear the Socialists apart, either by a frontal assault or by absorption, or it works in the opposite direction with the same intensity to bring about a Socialist resurrection. But it is not enough simply that there are Socialists. There has to be a Socialist party that meets two criteria: (1) it must be susceptible to forming an alliance with the Communists—a left-Socialist party rather than a social-democratic Socialist party, and (2) in a coalition of the Left it must appear to be the strongest vote-getter among the coalition members.

Although Thorez himself made the decision in 1962 to return to a Popular Front strategy, its implementation was blocked for a long time, at first by the social-democratization of the SFIO [French Section of the Workers International, the traditional Socialist party in France] under Guy Mollet and then by the weakness and near-liquidation of the Socialist party prior to 1969. The FCP could well have done what the ICP did, which was to express satisfaction more or less secretly when the Italian Socialist party disappeared. The Italian Communists had fought, scorned, and hated the Socialists, and they had no trouble adjusting to the party's end. On the contrary, at the end of the 1960s the FCP showed that it firmly hoped to see the regrowth of a large Socialist party.

This hope was based on history. One of the charms of the French Socialist party is its capacity to astonish profoundly those who mourn its definitive demise. Indeed, on three occasions in hardly half a century it has died, or, at least, it fell so low as to give the impression that it was about to take its last breath. But on three occasions the last breath somehow revived it and fired it up.

It must be said that the FCP certainly played a role in saving and reviving the Socialist party, especially by lowering its demands regarding the conditions on which it would make an alliance that would restore vigor and credibility to its ally. Naturally enough, the Socialist party had to pay a high price, and in addition it had to accept, through the intermediary of its left wing, a Leninist analytic framework that would reinforce the alliance through similarities in doctrine and in type of language.

Here we find the double paradox of French socialism since 1920. First, French socialism can develop only in the shadow and under the theoretical and semantic influence of its Communist neighbor, either in alliance or in opposition but always in a symbiotic relationship. Second, although the first paradox excludes it from being a social-democratic party and makes it rather a leftist party, it must also be a heterogeneous Socialist party—and therefore be internally fragile—because while it needs a left wing to keep in contact with the Communist party it also needs a right wing to keep in contact with the voters, who will make it the dominant party within the coalition.

Two attempts were made before this long and risky job was successfully launched. It was only in 1969 that a Socialist party took shape with the youthful vigor that gave rise to positive expectations.

In order to accelerate the Socialist development, the French Communist party took one more step forward: it proposed the elaboration of a "Common Program." There were two advantages in this for the FCP: in the short run, this program would furnish the basis for the alliance and would speed up the Socialist recovery; and in the long run, it would serve as a reference point likely to enliven and channel the alliance if it were to become a governmental alliance. It was with the Common Program in mind that the FCP formulated its own program in 1968 as a kind of curtain raiser and stimulant—the Champigny Program, which took its name from the Paris suburb where the Central Committee adopted it. The Champigny Program was intended to serve as the background for the Socialist-Communist conversations, which ended in agreement in 1972. The Common Program was not, after all, intended to be merely a duplication, rephrasing, or delayed version of the Communist program, but rather a document that would be compatible with the larger and more ambitious Champigny document.

It was then, and only then, that the FCP took on Eurocommunist coloration. At the beginning of the 1970s, when the party successfully concluded the operations described above—the contribution to Socialist renewal, elaboration of the Champigny Program, and negotiations for the establishment of the Common Program—it was going through a phase that cannot really be said to mark its inevitable conversion to Eurocommunism. Moreover, this was doubtless a moment when relations with the ICP were at their worst: the FCP's deliberate return to the classic frontist strategy, implying aid to the Socialist party and renegotiation of an alliance with it, was an "orthodox" alternative that contrasted with the new Italian strategy of the historic compromise. But just as it had been necessary in the mid-1930s for the frontist strategy to become as broad and effective as possible, to go beyond mere tactical political changes to the stage of doctrinal changes themselves, in the mid-1970s the FCP found it necessary to reinforce its return to the leftist union strategy by revising those parts of its doctrine that were mostly strongly tied to the former strategy of "class against class" or "Cold War."

Which elements in Communist theory had come under the attack of Thorez in 1936? There were two important ones. While not abandoning the concept of the dictatorship of the proletariat, the secretary-general nevertheless abolished the slogans that constituted the cutting edge of this concept: "All power to the soviets" and "Soviets everywhere." In their place Thorez put a new slogan, "For democracy against fascism." While in no way denying proletarian internationalism, he nevertheless discarded the notion of "revolutionary defeatism," which had long motivated French Communists to vote against the defense budget, and he declared publicly, "We love our country." At the time, that declaration caused as much sensation as the most shocking statements of our day.

I think we would agree that the source of inspiration for the doctrinal changes being proposed today for the FCP is troubling. Georges

Marchais always has the words *democracy* and *national independence* on his lips. In a speech to the Central Committee on May 11, 1977, he said:

> The Twenty-second Congress has made *liberty* and *democracy* the principal fighting goals of the working class in our country. But the Twenty-second Congress is also influenced by another motivating idea of no less theoretical and political importance: *national independence*.

Just as Thorez had made an abrupt turnabout to accept the obligations of national defense in his time, Marchais has finally agreed to recognize the French strategic nuclear force as a "fact." The only difference is that he must pay an apparently greater price than Thorez in order to be credible. First, he has done more than abandon a slogan derived from the principle of the dictatorship of the proletariat. He has abandoned the very concept itself, which amounts to confounding blithely the order of theory and the order of strategy, but in an area where, and it matters not how, theoretical semantics is so confused that it's just as well to wipe the slate clean.

One advantage of this is that it would no longer be necessary to provide lengthy explanations to people who, having maintained some shred of Marxist thinking, express concern about the date of the eventual disappearance of the state in the socialist countries. They have not noticed that there can hardly be a withering away of the state where there is no state—but instead a party that has absorbed all functions both of the state and of civil society.

On the other hand, if, like Thorez, Marchais does not renounce proletarian internationalism, which is not an abstract concept but the very soul of communism, he must at least in the short run get into open arguments with Brezhnev. Thorez limited himself to saying with a straight face that French Communist policy was established in Paris, not in Moscow. What is at stake here is both the increase in the degree of anti-Sovietism necessary today to give credibility to a policy of national independence and the correlative degree of autonomy engendered when the favorable development of a process encourages the national figures to free themselves from the control of the international Communist movement.

If I have correctly focused on the right dates and events, this summary permits us to see how French Eurocommunism is bound up with the deployment of the Union of the Left strategy—even if, by chance, it is motivated by other considerations and other ambitions, which remains to be proved. It is so bound up with the alliance that it runs the risk of becoming nothing more than a dimension of this strategy, in the long run becoming absorbed by it, so that Eurocommunism will be nothing more than the alliance itself. This strategy, we should recall, was created by the Stalinist period of the international Communist movement; it was characteristic of the 1930s and 1940s, the peak of Stalin's rule. Moreover, it was Stalin who taught the Communist parties how to use this strategy wisely; conceived in 1932, developed in 1934, and institutionalized in 1936, it was brutally rejected in 1939. It was then taken out of storage in 1941, put back into use in 1943, and once again rejected in 1947.

And the Communists can neither cover up nor hide from themselves this embarrassing coincidence between the Popular Front and the high point of Stalinism. But they try nevertheless to rewrite history to suit themselves, in spite of their pronounced love of truth. Thus we find Claude Prévost writing in *L'Humanité* (April 2, 1977)—in a column reprinted without comment by *Le Monde*—in the mold of the "late Marburg political expert, Werner Hofmann," saying that "the Popular Front-type strategy represents a *substantive break* with Stalinism." Substantive? Surely, but Stalin apparently recovered quite well after this rupture with himself, if one judges by the length of his rule (1924–53). And Prévost added, "According to different sources, what we now know about the first meetings of the Cominform after the war confirms that the Popular Front strategy and the National Front-type developments during the Resistance and the Liberation in France and Italy were never really accepted by what we call 'Stalinism.'" Really? This *L'Humanité* columnist is disappointed that we don't know our history better. Not at all; we know the history. It just doesn't have the same meaning that Claude Prévost wrings out of it to support his point.

Were there many lively and intense discussions inside the party before the adoption of the new strategy at the beginning of the 1930s? But of course. Even under Stalin there were discussions. It was not forbidden to any Communist party—called sections of the Communist International— to take note of new developments before the Executive Committee of the Comintern did so. Nevertheless, it was understood that Stalin would have the last word, and it was wise for each participant in the discussion to guess as early as possible which side was going to win. Were there some harsh retrospective exchanges in 1947 at the expense of the French and Italian parties, before Tito repaid a hundredfold the pleasures he had in ridiculing them? But those were typical Stalinist games—how else could the passage from one strategy to another be camouflaged? Too bad for those who believed naïvely that the "patriotic and democratic" jargon of the Resistance years had suddenly become the alpha and omega of Marxism, and who consequently improperly pushed into the theoretical plane what was only strategic.

There is a considerable margin between that position and acceptance of the sugar-coated version of the Stalinist dictatorship that Prévost wants us to buy. For according to Prévost, far from being the blood-thirsty dictator, as he is generally described, Stalin would thus have allowed himself to be challenged and defeated in the 1930s by the daring "frontists" of the French Communist party. Well, there would still remain the famous "Stalin was right" to explain, the motto that appeared on the walls of France, one spring night in 1935, to sanction after the fact the shocking acceptance by the FCP of the national defense policy that Laval and Stalin had just conferred about and agreed upon.

Once again this is an attempt to cut things into slices: Thorez and the French Communist party get the Popular Front of 1936; Stalin gets the purge trials and the mass terror of the same year. Unfortunately, history doesn't lend itself to being cut into slices. The Communist world directed by Stalin in 1936 was *simultaneously* the Popular Front and the purge trials. And Thorez was simultaneously the gifted and happy artisan of the Popular Front and the "best French Stalinist."

III.

This leads us to wonder whether the Eurocommunist dimension comes into play more at the following stage in the process: the moment after the electoral victory when it becomes time to judge what the chances are that a Union of the Left government can implement its program. There, also, we must make some distinctions.

Are the chances of a leftist government to govern successfully—in general, in conformity with its program—increased by the fact that the FCP considers itself motivated by Eurocommunist intentions?

Perhaps so, because the Communist party has indeed renounced using means that would jeopardize the gains of democracy. Since citizens of goodwill might consider this a guarantee, it is likely to sway them to show more confidence in the Communists than they have done before.

But the effect will nevertheless be limited, because the Communists and Socialists will have received the mandate to apply not a Eurocommunist policy but the Common Program, which was conceived of before the Eurocommunization of the FCP. It is this Common Program, not Eurocommunism, that must bear up under the difficulties resulting from an eventual electoral victory of the Left and the installation of a joint government. These problems include an inevitable constitutional crisis; the lengthy problem of mastering the machinery of state, which takes its time responding to the orders of new leaders even when the transfer of power is between two governments of the same political leaning; the slowdown of the economic machinery, which will start even before the new government takes power, as industrial leaders automatically postpone any new initiatives until they can see what's going on; and finally the unleashing of restraints in a society that is tremulous with desire and expectations.

In fact, the Common Program is based on considerations that do not necessarily come from the same source as Eurocommunism does. The decision to carry out nationalizations, for example, stems from the orthodox analysis of the "general crisis of capitalism" and its most recent formulation, the crisis of "state monopoly capitalism." The key to this crisis is reputed to be the overaccumulation of capital; this is the thesis that was supported by FCP economists at the Stockholm conference in 1976, where European Communist experts exchanged views on inflation and incomes policy. The Italian Communists vainly emphasized changes in the market structure, both internal and international, as well as changes in the relationship of forces controlled by different classes in order to allow labor unions and Third World countries to impose modifications in their favor of "terms of trade." They vainly called for a "kind of incomes policy" to modify the relationship between production and consumption. Through it all, the French Communists remained faithful to the classic Leninist priority by which all control must go to the state, and therefore they supported nationalizations.

It will be interesting to observe whether the revision of the Common Program, agreed to by the Socialist party and the FCP in 1977, will show more evidence of the Eurocommunization process undergone by the FCP than the earlier version.

It is to another level that we must look, however, to find where the FCP's Eurocommunism might play a new role: possibly the Eurocommunized party would introduce new aspects into its conception and practice of a 1978 version of the Popular Front. These novelties would contrast not only with the conception and practice of the Popular Front in the 1930s but also with the Chilean and Portuguese styles of "Popular Union" in the 1970s.

The novelty would stem from the Communist renunciation, for an indeterminate but relatively long period of time, of considering the Union of the Left government as only a transitory step that, by means of an overthrow of the economic mechanisms of French society, will lead to a second, and decisive, step, during which both Communist power and socialist society will be established. In short, the Communists would behave as if from their point of view the Union of the Left is a permanent arrangement. Consequently, they would plan to support a Socialist-led government, but not the way "a rope supports a hanging man." Moreover, they would have to ask their Socialist allies to behave somewhat otherwise than they did at the time when both groups were persuaded that the Union of the Left government was only a first step that could lead inevitably to an internal struggle for the conquest of hegemony. This battle would have to end with the expulsion of one or the other group from a government that, in so many words, would not be big enough for both of them.

For the Communists to give up this kind of thinking means that Communist leaders would have to warn their militants not to be concerned if, after the common victory, the Socialists shamelessly grab the spoils that the Communists wanted for themselves. The FCP would have to limit itself to joint and concentrated actions designed to give it solid control, after negotiations with the Socialists, of the nerve centers that attract it most strongly: the centers that control movement in all its forms—energy, ideas, goods, and persons. What the Communist renunciation means, above all, is that the Communists would not devote themselves, in the words of Vaillant-Couturier in 1936, to the "ministry of the masses," leaving all the governmental tasks to the Socialists.

In sum, they would have to forego creating a system of dual power by strictly abstaining from the two preferred methods used in the past and still valid for this kind of situation: first, the installation of a second decision-making network based primarily on the labor unions, running parallel to the state system; second, the implementation of a policy of purges, either open or disguised. We well know what a policy of purges is: calling the Socialists to task constantly to show the proof—always insufficient—of their revolutionary ardor; making them drive out their own members—for instance, making them on demand purge beyond the pale the Left Radicals whose anticapitalism is suspect, the left Gaullists whose rallying to the Union of the Left would have been on the late side, and right-wing Socialists whose past class collaboration could not be forgiven.

By rejecting these tactics, the Communists would bring something new into their thinking, a factor that they have neglected for too long—the concept of *duration*. To emphasize duration would prevent the new Popular Front from fading away in less than a year, as did its predecessor of 1936 and the "Tripartism" of 1946–47, or in less than two or three years, as did the Chilean and Portuguese Popular Fronts.

Unfortunately the Communists have given no indication of what they have in mind here, even in their new Eurocommunized form. It is probably for this reason that analysts, acting with too much haste, perhaps, but using as best they can the limited information available, waste no time in speculating on the likelihood of a Union of the Left government's carrying out a long-range "peaceful revolution." Most observers would admit that the 1978 legislative elections—if held in the expected format—will have real significance by giving voters a chance to "choose the kind of society they want," according to the expression currently in vogue. But these observers point out that such an electoral choice may not mean so much in the long run. After all, French voters really like the theatrics of a spectacular election campaign, so long as not much of substance is changed. Analysts consider that the elections will have a message ambiguous enough to be interpreted in two ways, one circumstantial, the other more fundamental. S. C. Kolm distinguishes a minimalist interpretation of the Common Program, whereby there wouldn't be much of a change, from a maximalist interpretation, whereby the program's application would be simply impossible. Similarly, there is a minimalist interpretation of the electoral success of the united Left, whereby it would be merely an ephemeral and relatively expensive adventure, and a maximalist interpretation, whereby it would try to go so far beyond its capabilities that it would render itself too fragile.

The real significance of both a united Left electoral victory and a resulting Union of the Left government would not be clear from what happened immediately after the elections but would emerge from the evolutionary process that would lead the alliance to something else. Consequently, the real speculation going on today is about what the chances are of each of the four possibilities that might arise if France, having put a Union of the Left government in power, wants to "get rid of it."

Few give much credence to the possibility of seeing one of the two "catastrophic" ways of moving beyond a Union of the Left government, although these paths are not completely closed off. It is not out of the question, for instance, that a grave economic crisis could lead to massive unemployment, creating both the symptom of and the breeding ground for the same pathological situation that spawned the "fascist beast" in the 1930s. It would nevertheless require incredible obstinacy on the part of the Left, whether united or not, to hold on to power in face of the opposition of the entire population, who would see a primarily military and fascist coup d'état from the extreme Right as the only way of breaking out of an otherwise paralyzed situation. As for the radicalization that would finally result in the taking of power by the Communist extreme Left, transforming France into a kind of proto-Communist regime—that would require a rather improbable, quasi-total, and chronic collapse of the structures of both the state and society in order to incite the Communists to take their chances without external protection—which would imply preliminary transformations of a drastic nature in the European environment—and to risk an enterprise that might well, in case of failure, be their own grave.

The elimination of the two "extremist" solutions leaves the two middle-road paths to be considered.

The center-left solution would have Mitterrand acting in France as Soarès did in Portugal. But at present there are two conditions Mitterrand lacks. First, unlike Soarès, he cannot benefit on the rebound from a counterrevolution such as the one attempted by the Portuguese Right in the summer of 1975, with their village priests, pitchforks, and peasant-farmers. France has hardly any peasant-farmers left, no more pitchforks, and very few village priests. Second, Mitterrand cannot do as Soarès did and get rid of the left wing of his party. Soarès had to deal with about 10 percent of his party and he could run the risk of an internal schism. For Mitterrand, on the other hand, the Left makes up nearly a third or more of the French Socialist party, and he could not take the risk. The absence of a counterbalance on the Right and the presence of a counterbalance on the Left signify that Mitterrand would not be able to break from his alliance with the Communists.

Does it look, then, as if the most likely successor to the leftist union would be the other moderate solution, the resurgence of the center-right, as in 1968? This would in all probability be Gaullism in the style of Jacques Chirac, which would lead eventually to protests of "Thirty years is enough!"

Or would the outcome be something else as yet unknown? It is vain utopianism to be like the Portuguese leftist military officers who thought that the world of politics had the fertility and creativity of dramatic illusion. The choice has to be made, and it has to come from what can be realistically expected now; we cannot hold out for a miraculous solution that somehow had escaped notice before. Moreover, it is hardly sufficient just to choose, even if we should choose well. We must examine another question: What would the price be to go beyond a government of the leftist union? What are the terms? Which risks are greatest? The ultimate risk, of course, is political collapse followed by a proto-Communist system, but this is a long shot. Much closer at hand would be the risk of an economic collapse of short duration—but having severe repercussions in the long run that would impoverish France and cause conditions favorable to an eventual Communist takeover.

But we've already gone into the domain of what the French Communists are wont to call *sépéculation*: a special kind of speculation that totters out beyond its supporting evidence.

In fact, we haven't the slightest idea of the extent of the period the Communists might be planning for the Union of the Left government beyond the usual narrow time limits for this type of government (between several months and two to three years), because at present there are signs that Communist thinking is not headed in that direction. Far from trying to slow down the traditional pace of things—in a word, to give reassurance to their allies and the right wing of the leftist coalition electorate—French Communists seem to be thinking about reversing the terms of the dilemma. Instead of holding back in order to furnish reassurance, they want to speed up so that the dynamics of the coalition do not lie in the search for the smallest common denominator but in the fullness and ambition of the common objective. To cite an example, in 1936 the Communists opposed the Socialist plans for substantial nationalizations in order to reassure their allies in the Radical party, but in 1977 the Communists are pushing to its limits the nationalization issue.

For the Communists, the government that will come out of an electoral
victory of the Union of the Left must partake of pure socialism, not of
ordinary democratic reformism. As things stand in the summer of 1977,
this is the only coherent sense that can be made of the efforts of French
Communists, under the pretext of updating the Common Program, to
reinforce considerably the especially socialist dimension of the Common
Program and to eliminate earlier ambiguities that might cause it to be
regarded as simply reformist.

IV.

While Eurocommunism may not greatly increase the chances for internal success of a leftist government, could it serve to attenuate the
external pressures that might be brought to bear against such a government? This external pressure would, of course, come from the United
States and the Soviet Union.

There has been considerable speculation about what the Americans
would or would not do if Eurocommunist parties were to participate in
the governments of the Latin countries. Many American liberals have
taken the position that the White House should welcome the accession to
power of Communist ministers in Italy, because the Communists would
be committed to substantial structural reforms. Some observers have
seen in certain acts of the Carter administration—the issuance of a visa
to Elio Cabbugiani, the Communist mayor of Florence, and the visit in
February 1977 of two American diplomats to Jean Kanapa in the FCP's
Central Committee headquarters in Paris—the signs that the American
government has changed its stance on Communist participation in
government. It seems, rather, that these changes have more to do with
form than with substance. The first instance is in line with the White
House campaign on human rights, and the second is just an example of
the usual contacts made once a given party becomes likely to be a future
governmental partner.

In the early months of the Carter administration, the government
conveyed the impression that it would not block the Left from coming to
power. A State Department communiqué on April 7, 1977, stated that
"the United States would not intervene in West European countries to
prevent the participation of Communists in government." Nevertheless,
this same communiqué made it clear that the American government

differentiated between intervention on one hand and concern on the other: "We do not propose to involve ourselves in the processes by which they [the West European countries] reach their decisions. . . . This does not mean that our attitude is one of indifference."

The American government will no doubt repeat what Kissinger said during the Italian election campaign in 1976: the idea of Communists in the government is not a good one. American policy will continue to disapprove of Communist governmental participation, whether Euro-communist or not. [Meeting with Socialist and Left Radical party leaders in Paris on January 6, 1978, President Carter expressed great concern about the possibility of renewing the electoral alliance with the French Communist party. A State Department communiqué on the Italian situation, issued on January 12, reiterated the American position that "our Western European allies are sovereign countries and . . . the decision on how they are governed rests with their citizens alone." However, the statement continued, American policy "on the issue of Communist participation in West European governments . . . is clear: We do not favor such participation and would like to see Communist influence in any Western European country reduced."—*Translator's note.*]

While Eurocommunism's ambiguities and uncertainties lessen the danger that Europe will slide into the Soviet camp or into the sphere of Soviet influence, there are still many possible risks. And why should the United States encourage Europe to run them, especially if they're not really necessary? In Portugal, at least, there was something at stake: it was necessary to break through the obstacle that had kept the country from democracy and modernity. In Spain and France in 1936 it was necessary to struggle against fascism and war. But the essence of the French situation today is that the stakes are ill-defined. Would the replacement of a right-center government by a left-center government really make any difference? Would substitution of a governing team that has been out of power for twenty years for one that has been in power for twenty years really change anything substantial?

The Americans can say what they think: they have the right to do so. The American government is also free to draw attention to "impending catastrophes" and to issue stern warnings. Everyone has the right to speak out, as long as one says immediately, as the Carter administration has repeatedly done, that it is up to the people concerned to make their own decision.

The essence of the American position is that having spoken they are now going to wait and see. There are three reasons for this. First, they have had a chance to see in the past few years that "free" Europe has shown a greater capacity for resistance to Communist or Soviet attraction than it had been credited with. The prophets of Europe's impending collapse have been woefully wrong. Nothing at all like that has happened, not in Turkey, nor in Greece, Portugal, or Spain, and not even in Italy.

Second, although Americans do not like Communists, they have a special affinity for Socialists, and not just because the French Socialists are often more "Atlanticist" than the Gaullists, for example. The Americans share with European Socialists the same overarching ideas: priority for democratic freedoms, a militant sense of humanism, an optimistic vision of the perfectibility of man and of society, and a liking for tolerance.

The third reason springs directly from the contemporary situation: the Americans will bide their time, because there's no fire. Spain? No fire at all. Italy? Well, it's burning, but on the back burner. The present forms of connivance between the Christian Democrats and the Italian Communist party, while a bit uncomfortable on both sides, are likely to last as long as the Italian voters will put up with the situation. Moreover, the time is coming when the Christian Democrats will want to take advantage of forthcoming elections that will give them back the position of dominant party in Italy, which they have momentarily lost.

So it's only in France that a real fire could break out. The results of the March 1977 municipal elections gave a big boost to the Union of the Left's chances to win legislative elections in the spring 1978. But there are two unknown factors that might modify the expected results, in the absence of any completely unforeseen radically new developments. First, does the Right still enjoy the offsetting advantages that seem to accrue to it according to the importance of an election, whereby presidential elections would count more than legislative elections, and legislative elections more than municipal ones? Second, to what extent would a substantial economic recovery influence the vote, notwithstanding the fact that even such a recovery could not hope to overcome the two problems affecting the economy all over the world—unemployment and inflation?

The response to this second question is even more uncertain because the French economy has already rebounded to unhoped-for levels. The economic losses of 1975 have been almost recouped by the performance in 1976 and especially in 1977. Nevertheless, the public's behavior at the polls in the recent municipal elections showed that the electorate did not respond to these signs of recovery, no doubt because they were global and abstract: a good balance-of-payments situation is less visible than the number, even approximate, of unemployed in a given region. The political consequences of economic recovery are all the more important because contrary to what is generally held, the outcome of an electoral battle does not depend entirely on the candidates' ability to win over the votes of the uncommitted middle-of-the-road electorate; the most important people to convince are the hundreds of thousands of voters who are nominally affiliated with political parties or movements and who have not yet decided whether to renew or to break from their traditional political affiliation.

In any case, if the Union of the Left does win in the spring of 1978, the Americans will have some time to see what's going to happen; and there are many reasons to believe that they will consider it best to allow the French to work things out for themselves.

If the Left does win, what will its majority be? Will it pull in 51 or 52 percent of the votes, or is it likely to get nearly 60 percent? It is worth recalling that the Popular Front parties in 1936 received 56.1 percent of the vote, but the internal distribution of the vote among the parties was decidedly different from what it would be today. In 1936 the Radicals polled 18.1 percent; the Socialists, 22.8 percent; and the Communists, 15.2 percent. The expected figures for 1978 would be 30 to 33 percent for the Socialists and the Left Radicals; 19 to 20 percent for the Communists; and 3 to 4 percent for the extreme Left.

If the majority is only 51 or 52 percent, the new Popular Front will have only a lukewarm mandate for the next, and indispensable, step, which would be to make the president of the Republic, in this instance Giscard d'Estaing, "submit or resign." His resignation would allow the voters to return to the polls once again to chose a president corresponding to the new legislative majority. All of this would take time, and in the short run Giscard d'Estaing would have no choice but to name a prime minister from the new leftist majority and to work with a number of Communist ministers.

No matter how legal and legitimate these lengthy maneuvers and countermaneuvers are, they run the risk of being considered dilatory by those whose difficult personal situations and the belief that "anything is possible" as long as things change with dispatch will cause them to break out of their passivity and fly off the handle.

The leader of the Union of the Left will surely take the precaution of announcing, either before the election or as soon as the results are known, what his social and economic program is for the near future. But he will be somewhat handicapped by speaking before the fact, for he will not yet have any legal governmental power, and he will want to avoid the unfortunate and improper drama that developed during the crisis of 1968 when, on May 28, he announced plans to begin formation of a leftist government at a time when General de Gaulle was, of course, still the sole holder of legality as well as legitimacy.

It also appears likely that the Communists, even before victory is certain, would keep a watchful eye out and instruct their comrades to exercise restraint and to have confidence in the elected representatives. At this point, however, three elements come into play that might very well promptly discourage the Communists from recommending order and discipline.

First, while the extreme leftists of the 1968 generation have for the most part become good Communists, the foreseeable political and social situation will most likely generate a new brood of extreme leftists. In its youthful fancy, this new brood will certainly cause havoc, especially because the modalities of the Union of the Left will have obliged it to vote for "shabby" or "weak" candidates on the second round. It will want to convince itself that it is not resigned to a mediocre "frontist" alignment.

The second element is the inevitable gap between the spirit of the masses and that of the parties and organizations that supposedly control them. We well know that in bad times the parties and unions have to prod and pull at the rank-and-file members to get them to move; by contrast, when things heat up the organizations have to restrain and channel the energies of the masses to prevent their pent-up tensions from exploding in an anarchistic fashion. This alternating function of stirring up and cooling off is especially difficult in France because parties and unions are partly disarmed by the chronic structural lack of personnel at their disposal. The "net" that is supposed to hold in the masses and control them is full of holes, and the mesh it is made of is widely spaced. This is why the strike in 1936 ran away like a wild horse, all the more so since there was no rider to seize the reins.

What means are available to rein in a similar explosion in 1978? One obvious means is to prepare in advance a calendar with deadlines, but the Communists are no more disposed to consider a leftist timetable as intrinsically more preferable to a rightist one than they are ready to substitute a left-wing austerity program for a right-wing one. When they add up the various "fantastic" and "stupifying" campaign promises, it's not a question for them of playing a dangerous game that must be carefully handled to avoid postelection backlash. No, something much more serious is at stake. As their calculations have demonstrated, what they prove by adding up the sum of all the plans, programs, and reforms is not that the Union of the Left is more attractive but that the enormous expenses planned would in effect constitute a real and fundamental modification of economic structures. They want to prove that "it will be worth the trouble." As Roland Leroy has phrased it, the Common Program is "a mutual engagement for making things change."

And here is where the third element comes in. Things will start slowly and hesitantly, and the Communists will be able to control and channel the flow of events, but as changes begin to accumulate and the flow moves more rapidly, then, as they have always done, and as they cannot fail to do, the Communists will do an about-face and take things over. They will take this step even if it means upsetting the Union of the Left, because if the Communists must choose between the Union of the Left and the working class, they will always choose the working class, which is the source of their endurance and legitimacy, both in the short run and the long run. So the French Communists will not allow themselves to slip into the position of the Italian Communists, who allowed unemployed demonstrators to be fired on in the name of the government that they supported; unlike their Italian colleagues, the French Communists regard their identity as a workers' party, the party of the working class, as "the apple of their eye."

Returning to the question of external intervention, we earlier remarked that America would keep a hands-off policy in the short run. Is there any reason to believe that they might intervene in the longer run?

It does appear likely that a leftist victory would accentuate the economic crisis. The United States would react by pondering the desirability of rescuing the moderate revolutionaries to prevent economic disaster from radicalizing the country and condemning it to isolation in stagnation before it would join the Soviet camp. But the American

Congress would certainly not consider it appropriate to furnish massive financial aid in these circumstances; it would conclude, in any case, that aid should be arranged through multilateral channels by other members of the European Community. This line of reasoning would probably lead the United States to turn the matter over to the northern European social-democratic countries, who are better equipped to deal with the question. Once things had gotten so serious that there would no longer be any point in quibbling about the imprudence of the French Socialists in allying with Communists to achieve power—something already achieved without risk in their countries—these countries could decide when to get the French Socialists out of their sticky situation. The goal would be to get them out in the Portuguese manner, avoiding the Chilean dilemma. The more extreme the leftward orientation, the later the intervention would be.

The Spanish situation in 1936 took a tragic turn because of Caballero's Socialist party's revolutionary stance, the Chilean drama had its roots in Allende's Socialist party's exalted extremism, and the French Communists know well that the only guarantee they have against Socialist backsliding, which might take hold before they themselves had a chance to break off from their Socialist allies, is the power of their control over the Socialist party through its left wing, receptive to Leninist reasoning, and the intensity of the threat of a premature rupture of the alliance by the more moderate Socialist leaders which could destroy the unity and integrity of the Socialist party. François Mitterrand is no doubt well aware of this, as his actions to increase the unity and homogeneity of the party around his person and his policies have shown.

But these attempts have no more chance of succeeding today than Léon Blum's efforts when he also—the recognized leader of the Popular Front—hoped that he could emerge a stronger leader in the alliance than he was in his own party.

Here again is a classic paradox. The charisma of the leader of a mass movement seems to function better if he comes from "outside" rather than from within the group that he leads. "Outside" for Léon Blum was being a refined intellectual Jew, but as the heir to Jaurès he was completely within the Socialist tradition. "Outside" for Mitterrand is not being an offspring of the Socialist family, but he is closer than Blum was to being the classic model of a French politician. The key to this paradox is that because the demands of charisma make it imperative that the

Socialist leader have this outsider quality, he is not fully able to run the Socialist party's particular kind of structure. As Blum did before him, Mitterrand is finding this out. This is not because of the way the different forces play in the affairs of the party—which is designed to favor coalitions of groups and persons who want to conserve their autonomy within the party—but, rather, because the way in which a Socialist party is structured, from the ground up instead of from the top down. At the base there are groups, networks, circles, committees, support organizations, societies, and friendship links that are scaffolded together somehow to form a party that is neither a mass party nor a cadre party but a party of *factions*. It is in this manner that all the Japanese parties, not just the Socialist ones, are constituted. The term "faction" is more fitting than some of the other frequently used expressions such as "fractions," "currents," or "tendencies" because it conveys more accurately the relationship between elaborating a political program and obtaining a share of the power within the leadership institutions. This factional party bears a resemblance to one of those interesting and curious contemporary nursery schools in which each little class has its own shed, lopsidedly stuck up against, or over, or across, the other sheds, the whole thing held together by the chief architect's astute skill.

While the Americans might be willing to wait as far as economic considerations are concerned, would they follow the same approach in the military domain? Here is where the Eurocommunism of the Italian Communists could do wonders if they were to participate in a national union government. After all, the American military bases in Italy constitute an indispensable part of American strategy for NATO, the Mediterranean, and the Mideast. And it just so happens that Berlinguer, who is concerned with what might happen in neighboring Yugoslavia when Tito dies, no longer wants Italy to pull out of the integrated military command of the NATO pact. His interview in *Corriere della Serra* during the election campaign in June 1976 referred to Italy's membership in NATO as a guarantee against an eventual attack by Russian tanks. It is, however, necessary to look at the nuances of his position. The editorial in the March 1, 1976, issue of *Unità* stated on page one that it was "unthinkable" that the ICP would "accept the Atlantic Pact in its present state," and demanded changes that would weaken the German-American influence in the alliance, which amounts to a rewording of the ICP's earlier demands for the withdrawal of Italy from NATO.

Moving from Italy to France, would the Eurocommunization of the French Communist party bring any new elements to defense policy that would either calm or accentuate American concerns? Not really.

The French Communists, to be sure, did carry out a thorough revision of their military policy as part of the larger Eurocommunist-inspired changes aimed at increasing emphasis on national independence. Most important, in May 1977 they suddenly announced their decision to accept the "only real means of dissuasion that the country will have for some time," thereby agreeing to the nuclear arms policy that they had heretofore opposed.

Along these lines, while calling for a freeze in the number of submarines and for the scrapping of the strategic air force, the Communists have accepted the idea that the nuclear strike force should be kept up-to-date, implying the continuation of scientific and technical work designed to increase the range and accuracy of the system and to develop multiple-warhead capabilities. They have also suggested that France build an independent antiaircraft and antimissile warning system based on satellites and airborne radar.

These policy stands must be understood in the proper perspective, however. First, the Communists have said nothing about increasing the defense budget to pay for these innovations. Next, no sooner had they agreed to a nuclear weapons policy than the Communists declared they wanted to limit its use to strategic military targets, excluding its use against cities, which amounts to eliminating most of the dissuasive effect of the policy, since the Communist limitations would make the strike force capable of destroying at most 5 percent of an adverse offensive infrastructure. Finally, and most important, the Communist military doctrine "would once again be a dissuasive strategy in the strictest sense," meaning that it would be aimed at "all points of the compass." When we add to that notion the fact that the use of nuclear force could result only from a "collegial decision," it is clear that Communist changes in military policy, like those in their European policy, are designed to help them catch up. They are trying to fight an unpleasant reality not from the outside anymore but from the inside.

These findings are confirmed by the fact that in other respects the Communists have kept intact the two earlier positions that constituted the real, and unchanged, significance of their military policy.

First, the FCP wants to break all ties with the military organization of the Atlantic Alliance, which would imply that France would pull out of the air defense system of NATO and would end its participation in planning coordinated actions in case of eventual application of Article 5 of the Atlantic Treaty (in defense of the Western position in Berlin, for example). Second, the FCP continues to call for the simultaneous dissolution of the Atlantic Alliance and the Warsaw Pact, a gesture that is impartial in appearance only, since dissolution of the Warsaw Pact would change none of the Soviet Union's defense arrangements, established through bilateral treaties between the Soviet Union and each of its satellites.

So the United States has nothing in particular to look forward to regarding military policy from Communist participation in the government. But there are two positive elements that might make the United States feel more at ease. First, although the Gaullists have remained respectful of the Atlantic Alliance and have been careful only to limit it to what does not impinge upon the independent exercise of French decision making, they have not been easy allies. Second, if there is one area where Socialists and Communists are in complete disagreement, it is certainly military policy. Therefore, the worst that might happen with a Union of the Left government is that it would do nothing. The exception that might have serious impact on American interests would be if a very French kind of dynamics overtakes the Union of the Left, responding to Gaullist exhortations, and awakens the latent Germanophobe sentiments, leading to a complete reversal of alliances: from a begrudging alliance with the United States to an anti-German alliance with the Soviet Union. Needless to say, the presence of the Socialists in the Union of the Left, at least as long as Germany has a social-democratic government, makes this scenario highly unlikely.

While it seems that the Eurocommunism of the Communists would not cause any serious perturbation in the attitude of the United States toward eventual leftist governments in Italy or France, would it modify the attitude of the Soviet Union?

Many Western optimists are suggesting in this situation as well that, contrary to appearances, if the Eurocommunists come to power it will be a windfall for the Americans and a headache for the Soviet Union. These analysts have overlooked an important detail that *L'Humanité*, to be sure, has not emphasized, while not altogether neglecting it, either: the message from the Soviet Communist party on March 24, 1977, "warmly congratulating the Communists and all the leftist forces in France on the

occasion of the great victory they have won in the municipal elections."
The message concluded, "Soviet Communists extend to you and to all
the leftist forces in France the hope for continued progress in your
worthy struggle for the interests of workers in your country, for peace,
democracy, and social progress."

These optimists are merely restating the proposals already made by
the Eurocommunists. Take Jean Elleinstein, for instance:

> In what way could the political transformation of France or Italy cause
> concern for the Soviet Union? To my way of thinking the essence is in
> the formation of a different type of socialism from that existing in the
> Soviet Union and its neighbors. Let's speak clearly: a democratic form
> of socialism in France would constitute a pole of attraction for those
> people in the Soviet Union and the European socialist countries who
> hope for more democracy within the existing socialist system (*Repères*,
> March 1977).

"Let's speak clearly"? Elleinstein must be joking. In good faith? That's
doubtful, given the distorted nature of his reasoning. Before this French
"democratic socialism" reaches a level of consistency and stability en-
abling it to perform as a credible challenge and a workable model, likely
to rival the deficient Soviet version, the Soviet Union will have an ample
buffer period. There has never been a revolution or liberation that did
not wrap itself in the brilliant and joyous colors of freedom. This was
especially true of the October Revolution; in subsequent years, in spite of
the hunger, cold, blood, and every conceivable excess, there was a corresponding excess of freedom, a breath of courage and madness that
intoxicated the liberal intelligentsia for a brief heady moment. And we
all surely remember the rose-tinted Portuguese revolution of 1974.

It would not be possible to judge the merits of Georges Marchais's
"democratic socialism" in just the first few months; even if France has
developed habits that make it hard for the country to give way to spontaneous celebration—there could hardly be a whole year of festivities as
in Portugal, and in 1968 even one month of celebration began to drag
somewhat—there would be abundant gaiety, enthusiasm, and pleasure.

Is it really the degree of permitted liberality that should serve as the
measure of how one Socialist regime compares with another? We should
point out that the Sino-Soviet crisis and schism, whose impact on the

international power structure has been both significant and lasting, are not related to any fear on the part of the Soviet Union—a fear that would have no basis, moreover—that its ideological rival might be less totalitarian than itself.

What is the Soviet Union likely to be disturbed about? The coming to power of the Left in a major European country would be rightly considered by the entire world as a victory for the Soviet Union and a threat to the United States. And this reaction would be justified: hasn't the principal goal of Soviet policy in Europe for the past twenty years been the destruction of the European Community? This goal would be much closer with a victory of the Left.

To be sure, the American defeat might be made less bitter, and the Soviet victory less sweet, by the hesitant and tentative diplomacy resulting from the internal contradictions of the Left; after all, the government would be swamped by domestic concerns, and like any government deeply engaged in structural reform it would not really have an appetite for major international strategy. So, to assert that victory of the Left in France in the 1978 elections would be an irreparable catastrophe or a definitive triumph for either the United States or the Soviet Union is to miss the subtle shadings of the situation and to neglect the costs that would be carried over on both sides. But to assume that the leftist victory would be a dark day in Moscow is complete self-deception. We should not confuse the severity of Soviet criticism of detours that might affect the achievement of socialism in Western Europe *before* everything was prepared with the consideration that the Soviets would show *after* the time had come, even if what had been realized has some problems, like too much freedom, that could be corrected in due course.

Once again we register the fact that Eurocommunism does not make any difference. Is it not, then, just an insignificant phenomenon, a fantasy of purely academic interest, a cynical politician's diversion? That is perhaps the case. What is certain is that if Eurocommunism does fully emerge one day, it will do so as the result of a process of evolution that is neither on the same wave length nor in the same rhythm as the real political battle under way over Communist participation in leftist governments. To be sure, the two processes have interfaced during their separate courses, but for the moment we don't run any risk at all in answering the question "What will the Communist parties do if . . . ?" by

saying, "As they have always done," each in its own way. This is what an
expert in European affairs of the stature of Bruno Kreisky concludes:

> As far as I'm concerned, Eurocommunism is not, properly speaking, a
> global political phenomenon. Let me explain. The difference between
> the FCP and the ICP, for example, is really crucial. I think that the FCP
> considers itself an openly revolutionary party. The ICP policy appears
> really reformist, but in revolutionary clothing. . . . I think that the best
> stance to take vis-à-vis the Communists is to make their democratic credi-
> bility the litmus test in order to find out in the long run whether their
> pledges do not simply constitute one of these classic about-faces that they
> have accustomed us to (*Le Figaro,* March 7, 1977).

From all this we can draw two simple and substantial conclusions:

1. The Eurocommunization of a Communist party is not in itself sufficient to modify the relationship between the party and the state. There
has to be another dimension, which depends upon the configuration of
the Left in a given country, particularly of the Socialist party's likelihood
of responding to the offers of alliance proposed by the Eurocommunized Communist party. In countries like Japan, where the Socialist
party is unsuited to or unresponsive to the offer of alliance, no matter
how Eurocommunized a Communist party is, it is frozen into a situation
that makes it an important national force, but not a party that might join
in a leftist shadow government that would be an alternative to power.

2. For the moment Eurocommunism is a process of differentiation in
the international Communist movement that by itself does not modify
the strengths of the camps and the forces at the international level.
Whereas the Sino-Soviet split brought about a major and so far definitive
upheaval in the international scene, Eurocommunism has done nothing
similar. Every "difference" does not have the same weight nor the same
effect.

Epilogue

Epilogue

On September 22, 1977, the negotiations that had been under way since springtime between the Communists, the Socialists, and the Left Radicals to update the Common Program were suspended indefinitely. The breakup of the Union of the Left, for which all the polling organizations had predicted victory in the legislative elections of spring 1978, was consummated. Whose fault was it?

Has the French Communist Party Changed?

Has the FCP, which everyone says has changed in such a complete and abrupt manner during the two years of its Eurocommunization, gone backward under Moscow's pressure? This is the question that has been most frequently put in the press and the broadcast media. But is it a valid question? No, not at all. We should, of course, note with satisfaction that people are finally comprehending the international dimension of the FCP; that people now realize that the FCP has a twofold, and unequal, nature. By priority it belongs to the international Communist movement; and circumstantially it participates in the French political system.

But it is essential not to misuse this accurate understanding of the forces behind Communist policy in France. It is not proper to conclude from the FCP's belonging to the international Communist movement—a movement that has developed in the sense of increasing its ability to control world events—that Brezhnev has the will or even the power to impose his views on Marchais. And it is also not proper to interpret the FCP's bid for the beginnings of autonomy as the recent product of a

[This epilogue was written on November 12, 1977.]

conversion to Eurocommunism; the FCP has been making this attempt for more than twenty years. (We have only to recall the troubled relations between Khrushchev and Thorez.) It stems from the necessity that exists within any complex transnational system to assure its relative cohesion while not overly restraining the initiative and vitality of its component parts.

It is therefore useless to look for the channel that Brezhnev used to give Marchais an order like "The Union of the Left must be broken up. Carry this out. Dismissed!" There was a time when things happened in this manner, but not any more.

To be sure, the Soviet Union has discreetly and continually shown its preference for maintaining the present majority in France; it expressed its hopes in this manner to continue to benefit from the internal tensions that Gaullist foreign policy has created within the Atlantic Alliance. Above all, the Soviet Union wanted to prevent the accession of a Union-of-the-Left government headed by a vice-president of the Socialist International—in the person of François Mitterrand—which would create a kind of continuous Socialist front from north to south in Western Europe. Moscow has long held that the Socialist International is the most indigenous, flexible, and enduring obstacle to the penetration of Communist ideas in Western Europe.

So Brezhnev, the Soviet Communist party, and the international Communist movement all tried to restrain the FCP from sliding into certain concessions, or from jumping into tactical operations that were judged too audacious, out of fear that if these moves met with failure, it would find itself on the receiving end of an "I told you so." Moreover, it appears that after a period of serious internal tensions the international Communist movement, as at other times in its long history, has seemed to be entering into a new phase of rapid normalization since at least spring 1977. Like most normalizations, this one seems to be taking place, if not at a middle position, then at least at a position that integrates what was accomplished during the recent crisis. The FCP will no longer have to take whatever the Communist world dishes out. It can show signs of the kind of independence that does not jeopardize its belonging to the Communist world.

Here is one concrete example. Marchais recently stated on television: "If in some absurd hypothesis the USSR committed an aggression against France, we would be in the front ranks to defend the national territory." Immediately good-natured souls would turn and say, "See, they have changed, and it's just out of spite that you won't accept it. Remember the famous Thorez statement in 1949, 'The French people will not, will never go to war against the Soviet Union'?" Unfortunately even the most cursory analysis reveals that these statements are in no way as different as some would wish: Marchais did not speak of *war*; he talked of *aggression*. While war is fairly easy to determine, aggression is a matter of interpretation.

So one should really stop wondering about the "changes" within the FCP. It is necessary to realize once and for all that the FCP is a Communist party; there is nothing in its acts or its own statements that could lead one to think that it has ceased being Communist. We have to recognize that it has never stopped proclaiming its unshakable attachment to communism. After we have recognized these fundamental facts about the FCP, and within the limits established by these facts, we can watch with interest the countless necessary and continuing changes that must take place within any organization, because it is through these changes that an organization can adapt to reality and to its environment.

Why Didn't the Socialist Party Give Way?

The Communist strategy for the Popular Front (or for the Union of the Left) involves two necessary and equally important things. First, there has to be an alliance between the Communists and the Socialists; second, the Communists must take the leadership of this alliance.

By leadership I refer to *political* leadership. It might well be, as was the case in 1936 and even in 1946, that the Socialists hold *electoral* leadership and thus leadership in the *government*. But what the Communists would not concede is control over the platform that serves as the basis for the alliance and constitutes the shared point of reference.

It was foreseeable, then, that after the municipal elections in March 1977 the Communists would launch the phase of their operation that would allow them to take over political leadership. Consequently, it would be wrong to point to a supposed decision to take a hard line that would have been made either last spring, during the "adding up the costs of the Common Program," or at the end of July or the beginning of August, after Georges Marchais's return from his vacation in Corsica, that would have led to the rupture in September. The truth is that there was no hardening of the Communist position; instead, there was a foreseeable and anticipated response to the demands of the situation that had arisen through application of the strategy laid out by the Communists since 1962.

The Communist calculation was that the Socialists would either give way, which was the most likely outcome, and would accept the Communist version of the Common Program six months before the elections; or they would not give way, in which case it would just be too bad—each party would "pick up its marbles." So the real question is, "Why didn't the Socialists give way?" After all, they had given way at each preceding step.

The first factor was of a *technical* nature. This time it was more difficult to give way because it was more difficult to hide the substance of what they were giving way on. In 1972 the Socialists gave way on a text—the Common Program of that time—that no one would probably read and that they themselves had not, it now seems, read very closely. In 1976 they gave way on the tactics for the municipal elections because it was complicated to figure out what the real Communist intentions were at that time. It was necessary to wait until after the elections to study the results and see what the Socialists had given up in the course of the thousands and thousands of separate local negotiations. This time the negotiations were centralized and public: they took place under the attentive eyes of the entire population, for whom thousands of reporters and analysts were working to explain and clarify each word and phrase.

The second factor was of an *ideological* nature: there was confusion in the Socialists' thinking that led them to overestimate the ideological convergence between the partners in the Common Program. According to the Socialists, the convergence had resulted on the one hand from the Eurocommunization of the Communists and on the other from their own abandonment of social-democratic weaknesses.

Now, that illusory convergence stemmed from a double misunderstanding. As far as Eurocommunism was concerned, it is not a variety of communism that differs in degree but in nature from the original Leninist matrix; instead, it is a complex procedure of modernization and updating of communism that serves to make it more capable of assuring its ascendancy on the societies of Western Europe. To consider it a procedure that subverts communism could only lead the Socialists to a most unfortunate error of judgment.

The other misunderstanding is all the more surprising because it is a misunderstanding that the Socialists have about themselves. Since they successfully rebuilt their party in the early 1970s, the French Socialists have persistently stated that they are not social democrats. But what does being a Socialist mean if it does not mean being a social democrat? To be sure, there are many different types of social democracy in Europe. It is possible to be a social democrat with a leaning toward the Third World, in the manner of Sweden's Olof Palme; or with a technocratic leaning, like Germany's Helmut Schmidt; or with a populist leaning, like the Iberians Soarès and Goncalves. But the common denominator is still social democracy.

Because the French Socialists lack a Léon Blum, who knows precisely what socialism is (for Blum socialism was really his *vieille maison* ["old house"]), and because they have rebuilt the party for the third time in 1969 under the watchful and hopeful eyes of the Communists, ready to furnish them the ideological and semantic materials they did not themselves possess, the Socialists thought that they were no longer social democrats but were something in between social democracy and communism. Unfortunately for them, there isn't anything between social democracy and communism. There's nothing coherent, at least. While it is certainly possible to borrow a little here and there to create a political amalgam, the result is a fragile structure because its materials come from two different building sites.

By deceiving themselves about their own nature, the Socialists led the Communists to believe they were going to swing all the way over. But when a concrete question arose—the nationalization issue—things abruptly fell back into place. The intoxication of rhetoric gave way to the sober fact that the Socialists had for the most part remained Socialists. What is the irreducible difference between socialism and communism? It was eighty years ago that the father of academic sociology, Émile Durkheim, who was a socialist by conviction if not by membership, and a good friend of Jaurès, wrote:

> While communism treats economic arrangements properly speaking as ancillary and changes them only where necessary to align them with its principle, the abolition of private property, socialism by contrast interferes with private property indirectly, and only when necessary to change it in order to align it with the fundamental economic rearrangements that are at the heart of its demands.

And that is the crux of the matter. On the subject of nationalizations, the Socialists talk of the economy, economic readjustments, and the creation of overall equilibrium. In short, they treat the economy as the domain where socialism is apt to produce an original solution to the problem of coordination between society and the state. But the Communists, in dealing with nationalizations, do not speak of economy and say even less about economic equilibrium. They want to abolish a sector where economic autonomy is still exercised in order to increase the political domain of the state. They are not concerned with a state-administered economy as such; their desire to augment the power of the state at the expense of economic autonomy is because at the same time—or at a later stage—they want to diminish the distance between the party and the state to the point where, at the final phase of the conquest of power, the party becomes the state, absorbs the state, and transforms itself into a party-state. At that time the state would be nothing more than the obverse side of the party.

There is a third factor, of a *theoretical* nature, that must be considered along with the technical and ideological factors to understand why the Socialists did not give way. The theoretical factor is the most fundamental of all. The Common Program, in its classic form of the thirties, appeared to be a drastic remedy whose costs and secondary risks were probably not justified by the veritable nature of the illness affecting French society; it looked like the wrong treatment. The most immediate problems for France, in effect, are not those of social inequity; they are new and worrisome problems such as control of physical resources, the production conditions and cost of new resources (especially energy), and, above all, control of human resources at a time when the supply of jobs in production of goods that can compete in foreign markets is going down and will continue to do so, while the demand for employment in unproductive sectors of the economy is increasing and must be satisfied.

It is both the excessive and the untimely nature of the Common Program's remedies that explains the turnaround in French public opinion that began last spring, after the municipal elections had shown the threatening nature of the coming legislative elections. This turnaround foreshadowed the Socialists' hesitations in September; the pressure of masses would have been necessary to push the Socialists toward accepting the Communist demands, but instead there was silent resistance from below, which acted as a brake.

But a fourth factor, a *political* factor, was the determining one in provoking the Socialist refusal: neither of the parties—the Communists nor the Socialists—was dominant enough to make the other back down. To be sure, the Socialists have more electoral support, but the Communists, able to benefit from the great extent of their partisan and union support, have greater strength on a day-by-day basis. One group in this tug-of-war has stronger arms; the other practices better footwork. Between the two, the rope broke.

And Now What?

The Communists did not make the mistake of rebounding from the Socialist refusal by launching into an entirely new venture. To be sure, they have other strategic possibilities than the Union of the Left. They can use one that they have had on ice since its effectiveness ceased—the Communists hate to throw anything away completely. This is the strategy they will call the "historic compromise," because it will sound up-to-date and will please the Italians. It consists in reusing their strategy from the de Gaulle-Pompidou era, a kind of "peaceful conflict" with the Gaullists. This reprise will both satisfy the Soviet Union and contribute to normalization of relations between Moscow and the Gallic Eurocommunists.

But the problem at hand now is not one for long-term speculation. For the moment it is out of the question that the Communists might reconsider and open themselves to new concessions in dealings with their recalcitrant allies. Their only preoccupation now is to keep up their pressure on the Socialists and to avoid coming to a hasty conclusion that there is no possibility of persuading the Socialists to change their decision. They will continue to press the Socialists to reconsider, because the relative strength of leftist forces, while evenly balanced in September, might become outright unfavorable to the Socialists in January. How would that come about?

This could happen in at least four ways. The first would be if one of the parties is shaken by internal dissension. At the present time, nothing like that is happening. For the Communists, this was predictable—even if the turn has been somewhat delicate for Georges Marchais. But for the Socialists these first weeks of storm and solitude have been encouraging. The party's solidarity has come into play, producing internal cohesion, even if some of its left-wing elements like the CERES [Centre d'études, de recherches et d'éducation socialistes; Center for Socialist Studies, Research, and Education] are taking advantage of the situation to gain strength and get their own candidates nominated for the coming elections.

A second way would be if one of the parties experiences such a rapid growth that the difference in size between the parties creates an insurmountable handicap for the smaller of the two. The FCP has announced that by the end of 1977 it will have received more than 150,000 new members for the calendar year, a figure about four times that of average annual recruitment during the sixties. The party would have added new members amounting to just a bit less than the total membership of the Socialist party. Overall, the Communist strength would surpass 600,000 members, making the FCP four times the size of the Socialist party.

The equilibrium between the two parties could also be jeopardized by a sudden upswing in labor conflicts. The CGT is fomenting such an upswing now that it looks useless to wait until next spring for electoral resolution of the overall political situation. If labor problems heat up, the Socialists will be under pressure because they do not want to lose their share of working-class leadership to the Communists. This question assumes an even greater measure of importance because a more serious form of "revolutionary impatience" may well raise some new issues in France: the very young adults, those who are just reaching "political age," have not yet been led into the deplorable activities of terrorism in France, unlike the situation in Italy and Germany, because they think that socialism can be attained by the ballot.

But it is in a fourth way that equilibrium between Socialist and Communist strengths might most likely be decisively destroyed to the benefit of the Communists: the Socialists could be hurt in the very area of their strength—their electoral capacity. Here the Communists detain the ultimate weapon—so ultimate, in fact, that they hesitate even to speak of it, much less brandish it. They have even made it clear that they would not consider the question before the last minute.

What would happen, then, if the Communists, failing to get Socialist acceptance for what they consider their minimal government program, decide to work only for themselves not only in the first round of the elections but also in the second? The Communist group in the National Assembly would probably be reduced to twenty-five members. Much as this would be unfortunate, it would not be fatal; it would not be the first time that this had happened. But what of the Socialists? Even if we accept the hypothesis (unverified at present) of strong support for the Socialists in the first round, and even if we accept the further hypothesis (this one is more likely) that part of the Communist electorate would be faithful to "republican discipline" and would not heed the order to abstain, the Socialists and the Left Radicals would win only about seventy seats.

Would the FCP dare to do this? Would it retreat before the vision of a catastrophe that would bring the Left back to its low-water mark of the pre-1962 period? Quite unlikely, because it has become a question of urgency and of the highest priority for the Communists to test the extent of resistance that can be offered by a Socialist party that has "swung to the right," to test it in order to destroy it with the same energy that they used to help raise it up. Is this a suicidal policy? There is certainly the risk that it won't be the Communist party that becomes the "entire Left," as it would hope to be, according to the Italian model. There is the risk that the Socialist party will shove the Communist party to the sidelines, but it is not a serious risk.

When all is said and done, everything depends upon how serious the present economic crisis really is. If the crisis is superficial to the point where recovery or the possibility of recovery appears soon, the Socialists will have been correct and will win support for having accepted the principle of "riding the crisis out." On the other hand, if recovery is still distant, as Raymond Barre thinks, it is the Communists who will benefit most from their demands.

Might the Socialists then take the initiative and block the Communist party's use of its ultimate weapon by taking a real turn to the right and concluding agreements with the parties on their right? They would be running two risks, both of them fatal, at this turning point where the Communists, having stated that they are at the turning point already, are waiting for them. Justifying after the fact the Communist accusations, the Socialists would lose their left, and they would lose support on their left. They will not decide to do this. The most probable outcome of the present situation, everything else being considered, is that the Left will be held in check, and that the Unity of the Left will remain suspended through the elections and for a considerable time thereafter.

Index

Index